Suitably Speaking:

Homilies from a Catholic Deacon

C. Michael Stinson

Parson's Porch Books
www.parsonsporchbooks.com

Suitably Speaking: Homilies from a Catholic Deacon
ISBN: Softcover 978-1-951472-46-7
Copyright © 2020 by C. Michael Stinson

All rights reserved. No part of this book may be reproduced or transmitted in any form or by any means, electronic or mechanical, including photocopying, recording, or by any information storage and retrieval system, without permission in writing from the publisher.

Cover image: detail of a window in the Mausoleum of Galla Placidia, Ravenna, Italy. Photo by author. Back cover photo of author by Anna Stinson.

With thanks to my father, the Rev. Charles L. Stinson, whose sermons I heard with profit for 35 years.

CONTENTS

INTRODUCTION 9

ADVENT

WATCHING AND WAITING 15
   Mark 13:33
THE LIVING STUMP 17
   Isaiah 11:1
NOT BY APPEARANCE 19
   Isaiah 11:3
CROSSING THE DESERT 21
   Isaiah 40:3
BAD ANSWER, BETTER ANSWER, BEST ANSWER 23
   Matthew 21:28-32
A CHANCE TO LISTEN 25
   Matthew 21:28-32
WHAT'S COMING NEXT 26
   Luke 1:39-45
UNWRAPPING THE PRESENCE 29
   Matthew 1:23
TWO MODELS OF GIVING 33
   1 Samuel 1:24-28, Luke 1:46-56

CHRISTMAS

A SIGN FOR AHAZ 34
   Isaiah 7:10-14
DON'T BE AFRAID 39
   Matthew 1:20
WHAT WE KNOW ABOUT ANNA 41
   Luke 2:36-38
FULL BUT STARVING 42
   Mark 6:45-52

ORDINARY TIME

CALLING AND COMMUNITY 45
   John 1:35-42
NOT AS MAN SEES 48
   1 Samuel 16:7
SECRET IDENTITIES 49
   Mark 1:40-45

HOW TO BE A LIGHT 51
    Matthew 5:14
GETTING WHAT WE NEED 52
    1 Kings 17:7-16
BAD THINGS, GOOD PEOPLE 54
    Matthew 5:45
PATIENCE AND AHAB 56
    1 Kings 21:17-29
FATHERS AND FREEDOM 58
    Galatians 3:26-29
PEARLS BEFORE SWINE 62
    Matthew 7:6
IN THE BOAT WITH JESUS 64
    Matthew 8:23
THE WINEBERRIES ARE RIPE 65
    Matthew 9:37-38
GOOD WORKERS NEEDED 67
    Matthew 9:37-38
PUTTING THE SHEEP FIRST 68
    Mark 6:34
RECOGNIZING THE TRINITY 72
    Genesis 18:1-10
STRETCHING OUT HIS HAND 76
    Exodus 14:21-27, 15:12; Matthew 12:49
THE GOD WHO REMOVES GUILT 77
    Micah 7:18
DOING THE IMPOSSIBLE 79
    Judges 6:11-24a
NO COSTUME IS GOOD ENOUGH 81
    Ezekiel 28:2
COMMUNITY, COMMUNION, AND THE OLYMPICS 83
    Luke 13:29
ALWAYS TIME TO PRAY 87
    Luke 6:12
WE'RE ALL TEACHERS 88
    Mark 9:31-32
BEING A GOOD DOG 91
    Luke 16:13
FROM MISERY TO FAITH 94
    Habakkuk 1:3
JONAH'S SECOND CHANCE 98
    Jonah 3:1-10

NOT CHANGING WHAT CAN'T BE CHANGED 100
   Matthew 22:15-21
UNITY IN THE TRINITY 103
   Ephesians 2:19-22
CONVENIENT OR INCONVENIENT 104
   2 Timothy 4:2
YOU'RE BEING WATCHED 108
   Luke 14:1
WHEN SOMETHING GETS LOST 111
   Luke 19:1-10
SHE REACHES OUT HER HANDS TO THE POOR 114
   Proverbs 31:19-20
ZACCHAEUS THE FRUIT 117
   Luke 19:1-10
GRUMBLE, GRUMBLE 118
   Luke 19:7
LOOK AT THE CRUCIFIX 120
   Luke 23:35-43

LENT

PROPER HYDRATION 127
   Isaiah 55:10-11
NOSTALGIA FOR A PLACE WE'VE NEVER BEEN 129
   Psalm 137:1,4
JESUS IS GOD 132
   John 10:31-42
PALMS IN OUR PALMS 134
   John 12:12-13

EASTER

KEEPING A SECRET, OR NOT 139
   John 20:17; Acts 2:36,39
A GHOST DOES NOT HAVE FLESH AND BLOOD 140
   Luke 24:39
WHAT CAN YOU DO? 143
   John 6:30-35
SHEEP JOKES 144
   John 19:27, Psalm 100:3
JESUS OUR SHEPHERD 147
   John 10:22
PEACE I LEAVE YOU 148
   John 14:27

NO UFO 149
   Acts 1:11
FEEL THE BURN 152
   Acts 2:3

SAINTS

BEING A MOTHER 155
   Luke 2:19
DISTRACTED DRIVERS 159
   Luke 2:19
BLAISE, THE HOLY HELPER 162
   Hebrews 12:1
BEING WHERE YOU'RE MEANT TO BE 164
   Mark 16:15
PHILIP AND JAMES AND ALL THE REST 168
   John 14:8-9
SEEING CLEARLY 170
   Tobit 2:9-14
MARY, US, AND THE ARCHANGELS 171
   Tobit 3:16-17; Revelation 12:7-8; Luke 1:26-27
FRANCIS AND THE EUCHARIST 173
   Galatians 6:17
LUKE'S STORIES 175
   Luke 1:1-4
THE ONLY TRAGEDY 177
   Matthew 5:1-12a
GROW UP! 180
   1 John 3:2
NO EXCUSES FOR MARTIN 183
   Luke 14:15-24
THE HUMILITY OF ST. CHARLES 185
   Philippians 2:7-8

INTRODUCTION

The work of the Holy Spirit is essential if Christian preaching is to have its maximum effect. The Spirit should inspire a preacher while he's writing his homily (if he writes it) and while he's preaching it, and the people listening to a homily should be open to the Holy Spirit if they want to receive the full benefit of what they're hearing. While I do believe that preachers should prepare their homilies with care, taking into consideration the time they have available and other circumstances, and while I am interested in the nuances of homily preparation and delivery, our human efforts in preparing and preaching our homilies are no substitute for the movement of the Holy Spirit in the lives of preachers or the lives of those who hear them.

Just as the Holy Spirit can use a homily that is heard, I also believe that the Spirit can use the text of a homily that is read. A printed homily text is analogous to a play script. The purpose of a play's script is to tell the actors what to say, and often to give some indication about how to say it. Reading the script is no substitute for seeing the play performed. The play's the thing; the script is subordinate to the performance. Likewise, the purpose of a written homily is to tell the preacher what to say, and perhaps to give some indication about how he should say it. Reading the homily is no substitute for hearing the homily delivered in its intended liturgical context. The liturgy's the thing, especially if it's the Mass; the homily is only a part of the Mass, and always subordinate to the Real Presence of Jesus. But we do read play scripts and benefit from doing so. And we can read homilies and benefit from doing so as well. And just as I believe the Holy Spirit is the key to people benefiting from a homily that they hear, I also believe that the Holy Spirit can use a printed homily when it is read, as long as its readers are open to the Spirit's movement.

The New Testament shows us that preaching has been characteristic of the Christian witness since the beginning of the Church, and the Church has known for 2000 years that the Holy Spirit uses preaching to move people. She has also known that the same Holy Spirit who inspires people when they hear a homily preached can use the written words of a homily to inspire them outside the liturgical context in which a homily was first delivered. Christians have not only been hearing homilies since the first Pentecost, they have been reading the homilies of their preachers for nearly 2000 years as well, so we know from experience that although homilies are first of all meant to be heard, they can also be of some use when they're encountered in printed form. I hope that this will be true for the homily texts printed here.

I was ordained a permanent deacon for the Diocese of Richmond, Virginia in October 2013, and one of the great privileges and pleasures of being a deacon has been preaching during Mass and occasionally during other liturgies. Before my ordination, I eagerly anticipated preaching as a deacon, both because of my great respect for the 2000-year heritage of Christian preaching and because of my own fortune in growing up in an environment that valued good preaching. Since my ordination, I've been blessed by opportunities to preach with some regularity. I preached the homilies in this volume during the first few years after my ordination, so in some sense they are a record of how I learned to preach; I hope that does not limit their usefulness. I've had the additional privilege of working with the Dominican friars from St. Thomas Aquinas Priory in Charlottesville, Virginia, who serve my home parish, St. George, in Scottsville. They have encouraged me as a preacher from the beginning of my time as a deacon, and since the Dominicans are properly the Order of Preachers, having not merely their permission but also their active encouragement has meant a great deal to me. This encouragement has come from my first pastor at St. George, Fr. Luke Clark, O.P., our current pastor, Fr. Joseph Barranger, O.P., and from many other friars who have served our parish. And of course when I'm not preaching myself, their presence at St. George means that I get to hear good Dominican preaching at Mass.

Adding to the encouragement of the Dominicans have been the kind words of many of our parishioners as well as the input of my wife, Tanya, and our three children, Cassidy (now Father Cassidy), Jeremy, and Anna, who are all mentioned occasionally in the homilies that follow. Preachers who care about their preaching should value feedback from their listeners that helps make them better communicators, and while I appreciate every comment I get about my homilies from the members of our parish, it's no surprise that some of the most direct feedback I've received has been from my family. I often have to restrain myself from asking parish members what they think about my preaching because I don't want to seem as though I'm hunting for compliments, but I seldom show that restraint with my family. I'm glad that they haven't yet told me to quit asking, usually in the car on the way home, "how was the homily?"

I'm also indebted to Fr. John David Ramsey, former pastor of Our Lady of Mount Carmel Catholic Church in Newport News, Virginia (and my sponsor when I entered the Church); Fr. Sal Añonuevo, pastor of Holy Name of Mary Catholic Church in Bedford, Virginia; Fr. James Glass, former campus chaplain at the College of William and Mary in Williamsburg, Virginia; and Fr. Hy Nguyen, former Vice Rector at Theological College, Washington, DC, for inviting me to preach in their places of ministry, leading to homilies that I've included in this compilation.

The homilies included in this volume are grouped according to the major divisions of the liturgical year, beginning with Advent and Christmas, continuing through Ordinary Time, Lent, and Easter, and concluding with a section for the saints. Within each section the homilies are arranged chronologically by the liturgical (not calendar) date on which they were preached, which is given above the beginning of each homily along with the calendar date. Where I have included more than one homily for a given liturgical date, the oldest comes first. If no location is given, the homily was preached at St. George Catholic Church, Scottsville, Virginia.

As far as possible the texts printed here preserve the words I preached. I often make last-minute changes to my homily texts on the printed copies I use while preaching, and through the years I've kept these copies and have used them to edit the homilies published here so that they match what I actually said at the ambo as closely as possible. This explains the incomplete sentences, interjections, and other oddities that I would not use in writing that's intended only to be read. I've made a few changes in punctuation, and in a few homilies song lyrics that I quoted while preaching have been omitted due to legal reasons. I've also added footnotes at various places that might help readers get more from these texts. Bible quotations are from the New American Bible, Revised Edition, sometimes as it has been adapted in the lectionary.

A word about my title. The first reading for the Memorial of Saint Thomas Aquinas, Priest and Doctor of the Church, is from Wisdom chapter 7. Verse 15 begins with the phrase, "Now God grant I speak suitably…." On hearing this reading proclaimed at a Mass a few years ago, I immediately thought, "that's what I've been trying to do during my first years of preaching as a deacon – speak suitably!" Many of us have endured homilies that seem entirely unsuitable or heard parts of a homily that seem unsuitable in the midst of an otherwise suitable one. As I said at the beginning of this introduction, preaching an entirely suitable homily depends on the action of the Holy Spirit, not just the efforts of the preacher, so the appeal to God that's given voice in the reading from Wisdom – God grant that I speak suitably – seems appropriate for me or any Christian preacher. Would that all our words, homiletic or otherwise, were suitable!

ADVENT

WATCHING AND WAITING
Mark 13:33

First Sunday of Advent, 30 Nov 2014

I never wear a watch. It seems like everywhere I go I have a way to tell time – there's a clock on the wall, or in my car, or I can look at my phone. (Except in here....) It's funny that we call a watch a watch because we don't really watch it very closely. Unless you are really, really bored. Or really hoping the preacher won't talk much longer. Usually we just glance at our watches, then continue what we're doing. But a watch is used to tell time, and when we're watching, and waiting, we're very aware of time. How long do we have to wait? And sometimes when we wait for something, we know when it's coming. But sometimes we don't.

It's Advent, which means Christmas is less than a month away. And we know that. We're waiting for it, but we know it will arrive on December 25th. And it will come no matter what. It's not going to surprise us, no matter what some people will be saying in about three weeks: "Christmas snuck up on me this year!" It really can't; we know when it will be here, ready or not.

But sometimes we watch for things that we think are coming – but we're not sure when. I remember watching for something once when I was a little boy. It was night. I was looking out of the front window of our house, looking for a red light: Rudolph's nose. What day do you think it was? Christmas Eve, of course.

I was watching and waiting and hoping to see it... but I never did. But that was the only night I watched for Rudolph and Santa's sleigh. Why? Why not look for Rudolph on July 15th or March 8th or some other night? Because I knew the story – that Santa comes on Christmas Eve.

That sense of watching for something at the right time – even though we don't know exactly when it's coming – is important for Christians. We should live our lives looking for Jesus, because we know he is coming – even though we don't know exactly when. Yes, we know Christmas is coming, and our celebration of Jesus coming to earth as a baby – the Incarnation. But every year, at the beginning of the new Church year – today – the readings remind us to be watchful. And we are watching for Jesus.

Jesus is coming, though we don't know when. At the end of time, yes. We say that in the creed. The end of our life is coming as well, though we don't know when, and that will mark a change in our relationship to Jesus as well. We should be watchful for those things. But what about today? What about every day? Jesus comes to us in other ways. He's present when we gather here for worship. When we see an infant or a young child. When we hear the scripture read and proclaimed. When we receive any of the sacraments, and most especially the Eucharist.

We should be watching and waiting for the end of time, and the end of our time. But how good are we at recognizing Jesus when he comes to us every day? We should also be watching for Jesus in these everyday encounters. He will come at the end of time; but he has already come, and he is here. "Watch, therefore," be alert.

THE LIVING STUMP
Isaiah 11:1

Tuesday of the First Week of Advent, 2 Dec 2014

We know where a tree stump comes from, and what it means. A tree was cut down, and the stump is what's left. The tree is dead and gone – except the stump. But stumps can be remarkably durable. They can remain in a forest without rotting for years, and sometimes a new tree will grow from the stump of the old one. The prophet Isaiah knew this as well as we do. But what was the stump of Jesse, and why do we hear about it at Advent?

Jesse was the father of David and grandfather of Solomon, the two great kings of Israel. After their time, Israel declined, lost her independence, and by the time of the New Testament, it had been a long time since Israel had been ruled by a descendant of Jesse. The family tree of the kings had been cut down. But the stump was still alive. Jesse's family was still living, even if they weren't ruling Israel. And one member of this family was a young lady named Mary.

Prophets had promised Israel a new king. The image of a branch growing from the stump of Jesse and blooming suggested that one of his descendants would be king again one day. And that's what happened, but not in the way many people expected. Jesus, the son of Mary, was born to be a king, but he was not a political ruler.

As the gospels of Luke and Matthew both make clear, Jesus was a descendant of Jesse. Humanly speaking, he was part of the former royal family. But Jesus came to establish the kingdom of God, a kingdom for all people – something even greater than a kingdom of Israel, meant primarily for the descendants of Abraham. And the kingdom Jesus established is still with us – we're part of it.

Advent is a time of preparation and looking forward. Christmas is coming, when we celebrate the birth of Jesus to Mary, and ultimately Jesus is coming again, and Advent reminds us every year to look forward to these things. But it's also a time of remembering. Jesus is the bloom of the stump of Jesse that God promised through Isaiah. He was the son of Mary, who was the first Israelite to realize that the new king of Israel, and his kingdom, would be something much different than the kingdom of his ancestors.

Advent is a time for us to remember what Mary knew: Jesus is a king who can never be defeated. Many people saw Jesus as a baby, but not many recognized him as a king. We look forward to his return as a king who will be recognized by everyone. The stump of Jesse has produced new growth that was not what everyone expected. And this tree can never be cut down.

NOT BY APPEARANCE
Isaiah 11:3

Tuesday of the First Week of Advent, 1 Dec 2015

"Look at that!" "Look at her!" "Look at him!" "Look at that big pile of… stuff." "Look at all those Christmas lights."

We spend a lot of time looking. Looking at TV, looking at our phones, and occasionally, when we're not looking at a screen, we might even look at each other. And during Advent, as Christmas gets closer, it seems there's even more to look at than normal. Catalogs and sales and decorations and more. The sights of Christmas can be delightful. But how often have we heard that you aren't supposed to judge a book by its cover? And how often have we felt misunderstood because we knew someone was judging us by our looks, and not by who we really are, inside?

Our first reading from Isaiah looks forward to the appearance of someone who will have all sorts of wonderful traits, including this one: … "not by appearance shall he judge." And we know this one Isaiah was looking for was Jesus.

It's Advent. It's a time when we remember that Jesus came in the past, when we look for his coming again in the future – and when we celebrate his coming into our lives, today, as we live between these other two times in history. The Jesus who comes into our lives today is that same Jesus who Isaiah looked forward to. And something that's still true about him today, just as it was then, is that Jesus does not judge by appearance.

And we can take this a step further. Not only did Isaiah look forward to one who would judge based on more than just appearance – Jesus clearly taught this ideal to his followers as well. In John 7:24, when he was teaching in the temple, he said, "Do not judge by appearances, but judge with right judgment." So not judging by appearances is both a character of Jesus, and a character he wants us to show in our own lives. He did not judge by appearances, and he doesn't want us to, either.

How much of our time, our money, our lives, are spent – used up – because of nothing more than looks? Especially as we get ready for Christmas. How much do we spend on things to make us look better to someone else? or better than someone else? How much do we spend on things that we give to someone else, so we won't look bad? Well, it's not bad to look good. It's not bad to give gifts. It's not bad to be creative. And it's not bad to seek beauty. Creativity and beauty and generosity are good things. But judging people, or being judged by them, based on nothing but appearance is a problem.

Jesus did not judge people by appearance: he judged them by who they really were. And he has a perfect knowledge of who we really are, whatever we look like. When he comes into our lives, he brings his perfect knowledge of who we really are. That might sound scary if we're hiding something. (That might be a hint that we've been away from the sacrament of reconciliation too long – and Advent is a great time to return to the sacrament if you haven't experienced it recently.)

But this also means that Jesus knows all the things we wish someone would know when they judge us. And Jesus doesn't just judge us fairly – he goes beyond fairness. He shows us mercy, mercy that comes with a perfect understanding of who we really are.

This Advent, as Jesus comes into our lives, we can be glad that he's not judging us on appearance. And when we look at others, especially when we're about to judge them, we can try to look at them the way Jesus looks at us – with mercy.

CROSSING THE DESERT
Isaiah 40:3

Tuesday of the Second Week of Advent, 6 Dec 2016

Deserts are defined by one thing: they're dry. If you go to the desert and you plan to stay long, you'd better take some water with you. And tonight we hear the words of Isaiah: "In the desert prepare the way of the LORD!"[1] The prophet was referring to a time of captivity. God's people spent time as captives in Babylon, but at the end of their captivity, they returned home, to Jerusalem and to freedom. And the most direct route home, from Babylon to Jerusalem, was through the desert.

Every year during Advent, we hear these words applied to John the Baptist: "In the desert, Prepare the way of the Lord!" John was like an Old Testament prophet, proclaiming the way to freedom, and he was preaching in the desert. To hear John, the people had to leave their homes and go into the desert. They lived in a land occupied by the Romans – once again, they weren't truly free. So the people traveling through the desert to hear John were like the people traveling through the desert to get home from Babylon. They were both thirsty for freedom.

Naturally some people who heard John probably thought he was talking about political freedom – freedom from the Romans. Cross the desert to get free from the Babylonians; cross the desert to get free from the Romans. It makes sense – but that's not what John was saying. The freedom John was talking about was different. When the people crossed the desert to hear John, they heard about Jesus. Jesus was going to be their source of freedom – not new land, and not new rulers, but a new way of relating to God, based on love. And that's a kind of freedom everyone is thirsty for.

In Advent we're also called to cross the desert. This is a penitential time, second only to Lent. Prayer and fasting and almsgiving are appropriate now, just as they are in Lent. Make it across the desert of self-denial, and freedom waits on the other side. But this is the opposite of what our culture says, isn't it? Around us right now there's an emphasis on parties and presents and the number of shopping days 'til Christmas. That doesn't sound like preparation

---

[1] All four gospels state that this verse was essential to the preaching of John the Baptist, and all four use the Greek word *eremo*, which is commonly translated "desert," though it's also translated "wilderness" in some English versions. This word, *eremo*, is the source of the English word "hermit."

for a trip across the desert. It doesn't sound like people who are thirsty for God's mercy.

We're called to be like the people of God heading home across the desert to Jerusalem, and like the people going to hear John the Baptist preaching – traveling through the desert to freedom. And like the people who heard John the Baptist, our freedom is in Jesus, whose Incarnation we're preparing to celebrate.

If we remember that before freedom comes the journey, before the feast comes the fasting, before the drinking comes the dryness – then we'll be more ready to meet Jesus on the other side of the desert.

BAD ANSWER, BETTER ANSWER, BEST ANSWER
Matthew 21:28-32

Tuesday of the Third Week of Advent, 16 Dec 2014

All through the gospels we're challenged with a few basic questions: who do we think Jesus is? are we doing what Jesus us wants to do with our lives? and if we're trying to do that – how enthusiastic are we about it?

In the parable we hear today, two possible responses to God's call are shown by the two brothers. Like them, we can respond positively, but then fail to act; or we can respond negatively, but then repent, and do what we're called to do. These two brothers represent two groups that Jesus interacted with: on one hand, the priests and elders who claimed to be God's people, but rejected the message of Jesus – and on the other hand, the tax collectors and prostitutes, who (to put it mildly) had not made an ideal first response to God's call, but according to Jesus, were entering the kingdom of God ahead of the religious leaders.

Tax collectors and prostitutes were Jews who had business dealings with the Romans who oppressed their people. They were considered unclean and unworthy by the chief priests and elders Jesus was talking to. Yet the chief priests and elders in their own way were also cooperating with the Romans. The religious leaders helped maintain order in society, and in turn the Romans allowed them to maintain their positions of authority.

Jesus didn't say that the tax collectors and prostitutes would one day enter the Kingdom of God... he said they were entering it, present tense. Despite their habits of both fiscal and physical intimacies with the Romans, despite their shaky positions in society, they had started responding positively to the call of Jesus. They had started to change their lives and follow him. By doing this they were entering the Kingdom. They were like the brother who said no – but then relented and did what his father asked.

All of us here have been called by God, and we've responded, at least to some degree. But how enthusiastic is our response? Do we see ourselves in one of the brothers? or in one of the groups in Jewish society Jesus was talking to? While a delayed response is better than never doing what we're called to do, we should realize that these two responses are not the only possible responses to the call of God. Neither brother in the parable showed an ideal response, even though one eventually does what's right.

But we do have a model for an ideal response: the model given to us by the Virgin Mary. Her response to God's call was both immediate and complete. When she heard and understood God's call, her response was "may it be done...according to your word." Her entire life was lived consistently with this response.

Jesus hints that it's not too late for the priests and elders. He says that the tax collectors and prostitutes were entering before them... but not that they would never enter. It's the nature of evangelism – even when Jesus is the evangelist – that not everyone responds immediately. Some who reject Jesus today might still, one day, respond to his call. The same is true for our efforts to live the life God has called us to. We don't always respond immediately, but God shows us mercy and patience.

As we move through the last days of Advent, we can ask ourselves how our responses are like those of the two brothers, or the tax collectors and prostitutes, or the priests and elders. But we might also try to model them after the response of the mother of that baby whose birth we're preparing to celebrate.

A CHANCE TO LISTEN
Matthew 21:28-32

Tuesday of the Third Week of Advent, 15 Dec 2015

Advent comes at the darkest time of year for us here in North America. It would be a quiet time of year, too, if we could stifle our noise long enough to notice. As Advent passes, the nights get longer, and Christmas Eve is one of the longest of the year. Silent night, holy night, as the song says. But often our lives aren't very silent. It's hard for us to hear. We're distracted, and often what distracts us are the many words other people are saying, and our urge to talk back, whether it's in person, or electronically.

Were the sons in today's gospel distracted? Were their lives too noisy? One told his father he wasn't going to go work in the vineyard, but then he changed his mind. The other son said he would go work for his father, but he never did. Do noise and distraction do this to us? How often do we say we won't do something... then realize that God is calling us to do it, and we'd better go? How often do we say we'll do something for God, then we get distracted, and don't do it?

Advent gives us a chance... to listen. Maybe it doesn't feel that way, with all the noise that surrounds us. Maybe I wasn't the only one rushing to get here tonight, after sending emails, writing a homily, giving an exam, and meeting with the dean. But here we are. The third week of Advent. The beginning of a long, dark evening. And the chance to be quiet, for at least few minutes... until youth group starts.

We do have noisy lives, noisy in many ways. But God, our Father, has things to tell us. He wants to send us into the vineyard, and if our lives are so noisy that we can't hear his Word – they're too noisy.

Advent reminds us that we're waiting on one unique Word to come into our lives: Jesus. Thank God that he does come. God help us this Advent to hear what He's saying.

WHAT'S COMING NEXT
Luke 1:39-45

Fourth Sunday of Advent, 20 Dec 2015

So, now that everyone has been to see the new *Star Wars* movie,[2] I can talk about what happened. There's one scene in particular I want to talk about...

OK, maybe not everyone has been to see it yet. I guess you don't want me to tell you what's coming. No spoilers! Sometimes you want to know what's coming next, and sometimes you don't.

Kind of like Christmas. Anybody excited about Christmas? We know Christmas is coming. We know it's only five days away. But maybe there's a package under the tree that you can't wait to open. Sometimes we don't know what's coming on Christmas, either.

Think about the Virgin Mary in today's gospel. Pregnant, and traveling to see Elizabeth, her relative. Did Mary know what was coming next? Well, yes and no. She'd been told by the angel Gabriel that she would have a son, that he would be named Jesus, and that he would rule his people. But what would he look like? What would he sound like? What would his first word be? Those are questioning any expectant mother might have. But in Mary's case she could also wonder, how would he become a king? How would his people respond to him? Mary didn't know that.

We've heard the gospel. We know what was coming next. Baptism, preaching, healing, teaching, exorcisms. Conflict, betrayal, crucifixion. And then, resurrection, ascension, and eternal rule. But other things about Jesus we don't know.

Think about this: We know more about the life of Jesus *in utero* than we know about his life from ages 13 to 30. Suppose you read a biography of some important historical figure and there were several pages about his mother's pregnancy, but nothing at all about his teenage years, or the entire decade of his 20s. We might think that was odd. Well, the gospels aren't normal biographies, but they are inspired, so when they spend time on one topic while ignoring others, we can assume it's for a good reason.

---

[2] *The Force Awakens* was released on 18 December, two days before I preached this homily. When I started my homily with this sentence, our choir director, who had not yet seen the movie, stood up in the back of the church and started making threatening gestures at me. At least I knew she was listening!

The story of Mary visiting Elizabeth while both are pregnant is there for a very good reason. It helps us understand what was coming next – even after we've heard the story. It tells us something important about who Mary is, and who Jesus is.

One thing this story shows us is that Mary is the new ark of the covenant. We read in the book of Exodus that God told his people to make a special gold-plated container. It was called the ark of the covenant because one of the things to be kept inside it was the stone tablets from Mount Sinai, where God made his covenant with his people. The other things kept inside it were the rod of Aaron, who was the leader of the priests; and a golden jar full of manna, the bread from heaven that God had fed the people in the desert.

So how is Mary the ark of the covenant? Inside the first ark of the covenant were tablets that held God's word, and a symbol of his priests, and some of the bread from heaven. And inside Mary was Jesus – who is God's word, and who is the priest who offered himself as the ultimate sacrifice for his people, and who is the bread from heaven who still feeds his people today. When Mary went to visit Elizabeth, how well did she understand that all this was coming next? God sent Mary, the living ark, containing inside her the ultimate way that people would know God – as the Word, as the ultimate high priest, as the bread of heaven – as Emmanuel, God with us.

When Mary brought Jesus into the home of Elizabeth, there was a celebration. Elizabeth cried out, and John the Baptist, not yet born, jumped for joy inside her. And Elizabeth said to Mary, "Blessed are you who believed that what was spoken to you by the Lord would be fulfilled." Mary believed, even though she didn't know exactly what was coming next. What none of them knew yet were all the details of how Jesus would become the savior, and the ruler of his people, even when they believed he would. When they were waiting for him to be born, no one knew yet how his people would receive him.

Today we're waiting on Christmas. We know it's coming, even though we might not know exactly what it will bring when it gets here. But most of all, we're waiting on Jesus. He came to earth as a baby – vulnerable, and entirely dependent on his mother. And he still comes to us in a vulnerable form: as bread and wine, here in the Mass.

In one way we do know what's coming next. Jesus, right here, vulnerable and exposed, but somehow still God. And when we receive Jesus, we leave here carrying him within us, so we become a little more like Mary ourselves. Mary was the new ark of the covenant, carrying Jesus within her – but she didn't know yet how his people would receive him. It's the same today for us as it was for Mary. Some people believe, and some don't, and we're not sure why. Some of us who do believe have a hard time telling others what we believe. Some of us who do believe don't always act as if we do.

Sometimes we don't know what's coming next in life, and we have a hard time believing. Thank God for Mary, who knows what it's like not to know, but who always believed, even when the angel seemed to be telling her something impossible, even when she didn't know exactly what was coming next.

I do know what happens in the new *Star Wars* movie. I'll just say... it left me wanting to know what happens in the next one! And I do know that Christmas is coming, and I am excited, even though I don't know exactly what's under the tree with my name on it. And most of all, I know Jesus is coming again. Not just some day, and not just on Christmas day, but right here – today. But I don't know what comes next – how are we going to receive him once he's here?

UNWRAPPING THE PRESENCE
Matthew 1:23

Fourth Sunday of Advent, 18 Dec 2016

When I was a kid, I couldn't wait for Christmas Eve, because that's when my family opened the presents that we gave each other. And to be honest, I still can't wait. So, today, I want to unwrap a present with you. I thought about saying, imagine a present under a tree.... But then I thought... I can do better than that.[3]

So what's in there? Well, you'll have to wait and see. Because first we need to talk about the gospel. Today's gospel tells us about a present that we've all been given. It says that Jesus would be called Emmanuel, which means 'God is with us.' The name Emmanuel, and the promise that God is with us, is a present to us – the promise of the presence of God.

In several places in the gospel of Matthew, we're told that something about Jesus fulfills a prophecy from the Old Testament. And the first time that happens in the gospel, it's here, when we're told that the birth of Jesus fulfills a prophecy about a baby born to a virgin and given the name Emmanuel. The gospel text says that after the baby is born, "they shall name him Emmanuel." We might read that and think oh, it means Mary and Joseph. That's who 'they' is – his parents. Except... Mary and Joseph didn't name their baby Emmanuel, did they?

Because immediately before this verse it says that an angel told Joseph, "you are to name him Jesus." And immediately after this verse it says that when the baby was born, he named him Jesus. And that was a good idea. Because when an angel shows up and tells you something you should do – you'd better do it.

But then who was going to name Jesus Emmanuel? Listen again to the definition that Matthew gives us: Emmanuel means 'God is with us.' And who is us? We are. God's people. And we do call him Emmanuel; every year we read these gospel verses, and we sing that wonderful hymn, "O Come, O Come, Emmanuel." Christians believe that God is with us because Jesus is with us. We believe Jesus is God, and when we call him Emmanuel, we affirm that. But what does it mean for us? Let's unwrap it some more.

---

[3] At this point in the homily I brought out a box wrapped as a Christmas present and held it up for everyone to see.

All through the gospel of Matthew people call Jesus, Jesus. Because that was his name. It's a name the Church uses every day in her prayers and in her preaching. Meanwhile, none of the other three gospels mentions the name Emmanuel. For that matter, the name Emmanuel is not mentioned anywhere else in the New Testament. And it's never used in the gospel of Matthew again after this point, either.

But we haven't finished unwrapping our present yet. This is the very first place in the gospel that Matthew writes about how Jesus fulfills Old Testament promises – which makes it interesting to look at how he ends the gospel. In this gospel, what's the very last thing Jesus does, just before he ascends to heaven? He tells his disciples, "I am with you always, until the end of the age." It's the very last line of the gospel of Matthew. Emmanuel means God is with us, and the last thing Jesus says while he's on this earth is "I am with you always."

Sometimes people say that Jesus didn't claim to be God. Well Jesus was a faithful Jew who knew the scriptures. And he knew that in Exodus, when Moses heard God speaking to him from a burning bush, and sending Moses to tell others about God, God said, "I am the God of your father... I will be with you..." And when Moses asked God who he would tell them had sent him – in other words, when Moses asked God what his name was, God said, "I am who I am... tell the Israelites: I AM has sent me to you." And Matthew says that when Jesus was about to leave Earth and was sending his followers out to tell others about him, he said, "I am with you always." Jesus identified himself using the same words that God used to name himself. Which is one way to call yourself God.

Jesus said this to his disciples, and he says it to us: "I am with you always, until the end of the age." And the age hasn't ended yet. And he is present with us, right now, during Advent, as our greatest present, Emmanuel.

Advent is full of delightful paradoxes. We're waiting for someone to come, but he's already here. We're waiting to celebrate the appearance of a baby, but Jesus, who was that baby, has existed forever. We're waiting to celebrate the birth of a baby who made the universe, who made the matter that made up his body ages before his body was made.

Jesus said, "I am with you always," and then he left the Earth. Yet he's here, now. So our present, which is his presence, is also a paradox. And here's another one: we can open this Christmas present any time of year. And we can open it over and over again, and every time we do, it will be as new as ever, even though it has been here forever.

So as we enjoy this last week of Advent, let's appreciate the many ways Jesus is with us. When he left his disciples standing there on the mountain, after he said, "I am with you always," and then left — what sort of presence, or present, did he leave behind? Let's unwrap it a little bit more.

He left us the Church, and the sacraments, and most especially the Eucharist — which we call the Real Presence. It is indeed a presence, and a present, of the most wonderful kind. Jesus is present in the Eucharist, and as we affirm this at every Mass, and receive him, he comes to be with us in a unique way, his body inside ours, the present of the past made present, his presence in our present. That is truly Emmanuel.

Jesus is also present in a special way in the Word of God, the Bible. Read it, study it, hear it proclaimed, and you meet Jesus, the Word of God in the Word of God. The Church has always venerated the Scriptures as she venerates the Lord's Body. So says the *Catechism*. [4]

And along with the sacraments and the scripture, we should experience Jesus in one another. If we are the Church we're called to be, God is with us, because we're with each other. And being who we should be every day means that we pray, and that we're aware of the presence of the Holy Spirit in our lives.

Jesus told his followers that after he left them, the Spirit would come to comfort them and guide them. And not long after Jesus ascended to heaven, the Holy Spirit did come in a dramatic way to give life to the early Church. The Spirit inspired the preaching of Peter, and the work of others who gave their lives to spread the gospel. And in the sacraments, we receive this same spirit.

Every one of us is called to receive the gift of the Holy Spirit in baptism, and in confirmation, and every one of us is given gifts by the Spirit to help the Church. When we see them alive and working in the Church, we know... God is with us. Jesus is God. The Holy Spirit which he sent is God — the same God. And when we open ourselves to the action of the Spirit in our lives, we're opening our lives to this Gift, the one who Jesus said will guide his

---

[4] *Catechism of the Catholic Church*, 2nd ed. (Washington, DC: United States Catholic Conference, 2000), 103. Subsequent references to the *Catechism* are cited as *CCC*.

Church after he left, after he said, "I am with you always." So Jesus is with us. The Holy Spirit is with us. God is with us – Emmanuel.

Christmas is still a week away. But the presence of Jesus is a present we can open, and we should open, now, and every day of our lives – the present of the presence of Jesus, God with us always, to the end of the age. So now it's time to open the present.[5]

---

[5] I took the top off the box and held it up so everyone could see inside. I had written the word "EMMANUEL" in large letters on the inside.

TWO MODELS OF GIVING
1 Samuel 1:24-28, Luke 1:46-56

Tuesday of the Fourth Week of Advent, 22 Dec 2015

Christmas is almost here. We often say that it's a season of giving. Today's readings show us two great models of giving – Hannah and Mary – mothers who give away their sons. Mary would have known the story of Hannah. It's helpful for us to think of all the ways that Hannah was a model for Mary. It's also helpful to know that even though Mary was without sin, God still gave her a human model to follow.

Hannah had no children; she was labeled as barren. No one expected her to have a child. But she received a son from God anyway. Mary had no children; she was a virgin. No one expected her to have a child. But she received a son from God anyway.

Hannah promised that if she had a son, she would give him back to God. And she did. She gave him back in the temple, where sacrifices were made. Mary promised to do whatever God's will was for her son. And she did. She gave him back on the cross, as the ultimate sacrifice.

Both Hannah and Mary sang songs of praise to God that were recorded in Scripture. And Hannah's song, which was our psalm tonight, was a model for Mary's Magnificat, which was our gospel tonight.

Both Hannah and Mary made a point of taking their child to the temple at a young age. When they did, both encountered prophetic men of God who partly (but not completely) understood the significance of the boy babies they were meeting.

We sometimes wonder how Mary could have said yes to God as confidently as she did, with no reservations. One reason is that she knew she was not the first Mother God had asked to make an exceptional sacrifice.

For us, it is the season of giving. But as Christians, we're always being called to give back to God what he's given to us. Everyone's calling is a little different, but no matter what God asks us to give him, it's good to remember the examples of Hannah and Mary.

A SIGN FOR AHAZ
Isaiah 7:10-14

Tuesday of the Fourth Week of Advent, 21 Dec 2016

During Advent, as we hear about John the Baptist, and Joseph and Mary, and Jesus, it's easy to overlook some of the other characters who are also part of their story. One them is Ahaz.

Ahaz was the king of Judah, which was part of what was left of the nation God gave his people after setting them free from Egypt. But Ahaz was not a good king. He worshiped idols; he put a pagan altar in the temple of God. God sent the prophet Isaiah to Ahaz with a message. God told Ahaz to do something. It sounds simple: ask God for a sign. It sounds like a good thing, something we might want: a sign from God. But Ahaz said no.

Why would he refuse such an opportunity? Apparently, he was more interested in his own plans than in God's signs. But after Ahaz refused, God gave him a sign anyway – the prediction of a virgin birth.

We don't know what Ahaz thought about that, but we do know something else about him. According to Matthew's gospel, he was an ancestor of Jesus.[6] The prediction that God made was partly fulfilled through Ahaz, even though Ahaz refused God's call. He was a man who worshiped false gods, but one of his descendants was true God and true man. Even though Ahaz said no to God, he was still used by God in a way he couldn't predict or prevent, as part of the plan of salvation.

God can work around our refusals, our hesitations, our denials. But why should he have to? Why should we say no to God since he's God? Why should we say no when he wants what's best for us? And why should we say no when we have another example: the example of Mary.

Mary said yes to God, yes to something that sounded unbelievable – that she would be a virgin mother. The sign that was given after the refusal of Ahaz came to fulfillment in the acceptance of Mary. In the end, God will accomplish his plan. But what part will we have in it?

God can turn refusal into acceptance, a virgin into a mother, and sinners into saints. During Advent, or Christmas, or any time of year, when God says he has something for us to do, we have two choices: no, or yes. We could be

---

[6] See Matthew 1:9. Many commentaries omit comment on this connection.

like Ahaz and say, not me, God. But let's be like Mary, and say, "May it be done to me according to your word."

CHRISTMAS

DON'T BE AFRAID
Matthew 1:20

Vigil of the Nativity of the Lord
(Christmas Eve), 24 Dec 2014

The angel said to Joseph, "do not be afraid to take Mary... into your home." We hear these words often in the gospels, don't be afraid, and they're an integral part of the Christmas story. When Gabriel came to Mary to tell her she would be the mother of Jesus, he said, "Do not be afraid...." And then when Jesus was born, an angel said to the shepherds, "Do not be afraid; for behold, I proclaim to you good news of great joy... for all the people."

Why are these words so important at Christmas? Well, this Christmas, ask yourself whether your joy is mixed with fear. Because the message of the angel – the word of God – is the same to us as it was to Mary, and to Joseph, and to the shepherds: don't be afraid – there's good news.

The message of Christmas is that Jesus is born; God has come to the world in human form; God will be with us in a new way. This is good news, and if we believe this, and live like we believe it, we have a reason to say, "don't be afraid." Maybe intellectually we agree with this. Maybe we've heard this message many times. If so, is it true that we're not afraid? Or do we need to hear these words anew, to hear them spoken in the night, like Joseph did?

This time of year, we hear about the magic of Christmas. Well, some things are even better than magic. Jesus is not a magician. Jesus is God. And Jesus didn't come to make us magicians, or to do magic. He came to make us like him, and to do miracles. The closer we get to him, the more we become like him, the more we're able to live without fear.

I can't say life will magically become perfect when we open our lives to Jesus. There is uncertainty and violence in our world, just like the world into which Jesus was born. His parents and their nation were being ruled by a foreign army that enforced its will with weapons of war. Some places in our world are still like that. Too many people in our world are sick, too many are lonely, too many are hungry. We shouldn't pretend this isn't true.

There's a new year coming, with new challenges. Financial challenges. Relationship challenges. Sometimes just the challenge of deciding exactly who we think we are, and what we should be doing with our lives. The promise of Christmas is not that everything will be perfect in this world. The promise of Christmas is that Jesus came into this imperfect world and knows what it's like to live here. And if we face this world with Jesus in our lives, we can be unafraid, because we know that the reality, we see is not the only reality there is.

Joseph did what the angel told him to do. He brought Mary and Jesus into his home. That didn't make the world perfect. Joseph still had to make a long trip to Egypt to protect his wife and child. Then he had to return to Nazareth and spend years working hard to support them. Like Joseph, we might have a long way to go to solve the difficulties we face, both as individuals and as a society. But the real meaning of Christmas, that Jesus is with us, will help us go where we have to go, and do what we have to do, with joy, and without fear.

The angel told Joseph not to be afraid to bring Mary into his house. And we know that when Joseph brought Mary into his house, he brought Jesus as well. This is true for us, just as it was for Joseph: when we bring Mary into our lives and our homes, we bring Jesus as well. And if we bring Jesus into our lives and our homes, we can say, "do not be afraid."

This is good news: Jesus was born. Jesus is here. And Jesus is God. So, do not be afraid.

- Don't be afraid of the uncertainties of the new year.
- Don't be afraid of the imperfections of life.
- Don't be afraid to ask for help.
- Don't be afraid to say thank you.
- Don't be afraid to ask God what to do.
- Don't be afraid to work to make the world a better place.
- Don't be afraid to say Merry Christmas.

And most of all – like Joseph, don't be afraid to welcome Jesus, and his mother, into your hearts and homes.

WHAT WE KNOW ABOUT ANNA
Luke 2:36-38

Sixth Day in the Octave of Christmas, 30 Dec 2014

Only the gospel of Luke, in the reading we just heard, tells us anything about Anna the prophetess. We don't know a lot about Anna, but what we know is exceptional. Luke calls her a prophetess. Jewish rabbis recognized only seven women by that title. If there had been seven, this would make Anna the eighth, and final, prophetess of her people.

But when Jesus was born, the time of prophets was over. Israel had been without a prophet (or prophetess!) for centuries. Yet when the infant Jesus was brought to the temple, both Anna and Simeon recognized that he was unique.[7] They gave thanks to God for him and proclaimed the good news about him – they acted prophetically.

We're told that Anna was from the tribe of Asher. Asher was one of the lost tribes of Israel, lost since the 8th century BC, when they were carried into captivity by the Assyrians. Hearing that Anna is from that tribe, and is a prophetess, is like having Israel's past made present again. It's as though, when Jesus appears, the past speaks to the present, and looks to the future, in the person of Anna.

Unlike Simeon, we're not told Anna's exact words when she speaks about Jesus. But we know that she had lived a long life and had spent most of her life in and around the temple, worshiping God, praying and fasting.

She had waited patiently for God, and she was finally rewarded. When Jesus appeared, she didn't hesitate to recognize him and acclaim him. So Anna's way of life, rather than her words, is her witness to us.

We don't know a lot about Anna, but what we know is exceptional. It's enough to make us ask, when it comes to recognizing Jesus when he enters our lives, if we live up to her example.

---

[7] Read Luke 2:22-40 for more context, including the words of Simeon.

FULL BUT STARVING
Mark 6:45-52

Christmas Weekday, 5 Jan 2016

Everyone knows what it's like to be hungry. Even babies cry and let you know they're hungry. And everyone knows that if you don't eat, you'll just get more hungry until you do. We also know that if you eat the wrong thing, you can be malnourished, and if you don't eat long enough, you'll starve to death.

Spiritual hunger is a lot like physical hunger. If we don't eat well, we'll be poorly nourished. If we don't eat at all, we'll starve. But spiritual hunger is different in some ways, too. People don't seem to feel pain from spiritual hunger like they do from physical hunger. If they do, why aren't they here?

I know plenty of people who don't seem to be hungry at all in a spiritual sense. Probably you do, too. Plenty of people never come to Church, and don't seem to be worried about it. Even in the Church it's not hard to meet people who are casual about missing Mass, or studying the Bible, or having some kind of prayer life outside of the Church building. And if that's true, we can't be too surprised that people who aren't Church members don't seem too hungry, either.

Tonight's gospel is a story about Jesus feeding hungry people. There's a version of this story in all four gospels. And all four gospels tell about Jesus teaching people, and healing them, and then feeding them physically. He knew people had both physical needs and spiritual needs, and he gave them what they needed to fill both. The same is true for us, and for everyone we know. We have physical needs, and spiritual needs. But it's possible to be physically well-fed, but to be starving spiritually at the same time.

One beautiful thing about the Mass is that it combines physical and spiritual food. When we receive Jesus in the Eucharist, we have a physical experience and a spiritual experience. That makes sense because we're both physical and spiritual creatures. Jesus knew about hunger because he was human, too. He ate, and he prayed. And he didn't let the people who followed him go hungry, physically or spiritually. That's still true if we stay close to him.

We're doing well if we keep ourselves well fed, in both senses. And we're doing good if we pray for those who are not well fed, in both senses.

ORDINARY TIME

CALLING AND COMMUNITY
John 1:35-42

Second Sunday in Ordinary Time, 18 Jan 2015

You can't play baseball, or basketball, or football, or soccer, or ultimate frisbee, with just one person. Maybe you can throw a ball (or a frisbee) up in the air and catch it by yourself – but to play a real game, you need teams. And Christianity is the same way. You can do some things by yourself. You can pray and read by yourself. But you need a team to play the game; and the team is called the Church. The Catholic Church, and your parish, and any other Christians you know – you're part of that team.

But maybe you don't like sports analogies. Maybe you think they're trite and overused. That's OK, because there are other ways to make the same point. Instead we might just use the word community. Christianity, if it's being done right, is not a solo act. Christianity is something that takes place in a community. We're part of a community, and we should live in communion with one another as we live in communion with our God. When we receive communion, in our celebration of the Eucharist, we need to be living in communion if the sacrament is going to have full effect in our lives.

Today's readings remind us of one particular situation when it's important to be a part of a community. And that's when it comes to the matter of vocation. Vocation is the word we often use to refer to what God is calling each of us to do with our lives. And just like anything else in our faith, we need the support of the community to find and express our vocation.

In today's gospel, we get a glimpse at what three of the closest followers of Jesus went through when they were called to follow him. One of them is not named, but tradition identifies him as John, the evangelist; the other two were Peter and his brother Andrew.

When Andrew introduced Simon to Jesus, and Jesus called Simon by a new version of his name, Peter had no idea what was in store for him. He hadn't yet heard the words "on this rock I will build my Church." He hadn't yet denied Jesus, run away in shame, and then been forgiven. He hadn't yet preached the gospel to thousands of people, before being crucified in Rome. He had no idea that in 2000 years, millions of people would look back and consider him the first in a line of more than 260 popes.

And what about Andrew? He had no idea that by introducing his brother to Jesus, he was starting this chain of events. He told Simon "we have found the Messiah," but he didn't know yet what kind of Messiah Jesus was, or what was in store for any of them. Not only the crucifixion and resurrection of Jesus, and the spread of the gospel, but according to tradition, Andrew's own death by crucifixion.

Like Andrew, we're called to lead others to Jesus. And like Peter, we're called to respond to Jesus when others bring him into our lives. In our lives together, in this community, we should be alert for opportunities to show Jesus to one another, and to see him in one another. And like Andrew and Peter, we don't know where Jesus will lead us. We find out together.

It's often said that Americans are individualistic – maybe too individualistic. Too worried about their individual lives, and not enough about community life. Maybe it's true. When it comes to our vocation, we might ask this: do we spend all of our time wondering what God is calling ME to do, and none of our time wondering what God is calling US to do? And when I'm trying to decide what God wants me to do, do I ever ask other Christians what they think? Or do I try to figure it out all by myself?

This is a basic question in the Christian life: what does God want me to do? But sometimes we seem to get stuck on that question. The answer is not as obvious as we'd like. We hear that God has a plan for our life – and we wonder why we can't figure out what it is. Maybe we identify with the great Yankee catcher, Yogi Berra, who once said, "I wish I had an answer to that, because I'm tired of answering that question."

Sometimes it seems that our only answer is that we don't have an answer yet. If we feel that way, it's good to know that we don't have to find the answer alone. Today's gospel reminds us that finding a plan for our lives is not something we do all by ourselves. It's something that happens when we're part of a community.

Maybe you've heard someone say that something is obvious to everyone – except the one person who really needs to know it. Maybe sometimes that applies to what God wants us to do with our lives. If you get too close to a page in a book, or a picture on a wall, what you're trying to see gets blurry. But then if you back up, the page or the picture comes into focus. Sometimes it's hard to get the distance we need to focus when the thing we're worried about is our own identity, our own vocation.

We can't get away from ourselves – but other people can get as close as we let them, or as far away as they need to be, to focus on the big picture. So maybe sometimes they can see things in us – obvious things – that we can't see.

Of course this can be scary. It means we're becoming vulnerable to one another. What happens when someone says, "you would be a great sister?" (And I mean religious sister, not sibling sister.) Or, "You would be a great priest?" Or maybe it's not quite that dramatic – maybe it's just "You'd be a great committee member." Or, "Can you help us with something...?" That might not sound like much – but remember that when Andrew and Peter first met Jesus, they had no idea where he would lead them. At first, all they did was go see where he was staying that evening. That sounds simple enough – but it was only the beginning.

I've quoted Yogi Berra – now let me quote Pope Francis. In *The Joy of the Gospel*, he says, "...the Gospel tells us constantly to run the risk of a face-to-face encounter with others....True faith in the incarnate Son of God is inseparable from self-giving, from membership in the community, from service, from reconciliation with others."[8]

We are all members of a team. So remember Andrew and Peter. Bring Jesus to others. Remember that others can bring Jesus to you. And pray that we will help each other figure out who God is calling us to be.

---

[8] *Evangelii Gaudium*, section 88.

NOT AS MAN SEES
1 Samuel 16:7

Tuesday of the Second Week of Ordinary Time, 19 Jan 2016

Our first reading tells us part of the story of God sending Samuel to anoint the next king of Israel, who would be their second king, after Saul. God told Samuel that one of the sons of a man named Jesse would be the new king, and Samuel thought that Eliab would be the one. He's listed first, which might indicate that he was the oldest son, which was a privileged position in that society. And in the story Eliab was basically being called a tall, good-looking guy. And there's nothing wrong with that. But God told Samuel that he couldn't judge by looks alone.

On the other hand, David was also called splendid to look at. So it's not that good looks are bad either. The point is, looks aren't what God judges by. God is not predictable; God doesn't use our standards. Maybe this seems obvious, but the one who had to be told this in the story was Samuel. Samuel was a great prophet, he was in touch with God, God spoke through him. And yet he was ready to apply human standards to this important decision of who would be the second king of Israel.

Looking back, we know that David wasn't just going to be the next king, he was going to be a great king, the king who in some ways foreshadowed Jesus, and in human terms an ancestor of Jesus. So this wasn't just a minor decision. But God still had to remind Samuel: my ways aren't your ways. I am not predictable. I don't judge by appearances. Not when it comes to kings, and not when it comes to us.

The host that we use at Mass looks simply and is made with nothing but flour and water. It's a small thin piece of bread. But don't judge by appearances; it becomes Jesus, and it can change our lives.

Like the sons of Eli, like the host, God doesn't judge us by appearances. He knows what's inside, and he can change our lives.

SECRET IDENTITIES
Mark 1:40-45

Sixth Sunday in Ordinary Time, 15 Feb 2015

If you've read *The Lord of the Rings*, or have seen the movie version, you might remember that early in the story, the hobbits reach the Inn of the Prancing Pony, where they meet a mysterious character. They first see him sitting in a dark corner, wrapped in a cloak, smoking a pipe, watching them, and making them nervous. The innkeeper tells them that he's dangerous, and that people call him Strider.

But by dawn of the next day, this strange character has saved their lives, and is leading them across the countryside on the next leg of their journey. They don't yet know that he has other names in other places. Eventually they learn his true name, Aragorn, but it's not until the end of the movie that they see him for who he really is – a king, on a throne, wearing royal robes and a crown. It takes time, and struggle, for his true identity to be made known.

In today's gospel Jesus, who has just begun to lead his followers through the countryside, heals a leper, but then tells him something that might seem strange: "...tell no one anything...." Keep my identity a secret, Jesus seems to say. And we might ask, "Why?" Someone had been healed from what was often an incurable disease – that's good news. But though this is the first place in Mark's gospel that Jesus tells someone to keep quiet about him – it's not the only place. This theme is sometimes called the Messianic Secret.

A practical reason for this secrecy becomes apparent by the end of the story. Jesus can no longer enter a town openly because so many people want to see him. As we read the gospels, another reason for the secret also emerges. Jesus is the Messiah, but few people realize this. And those who do realize it – including Peter and the other apostles – don't realize what kind of Messiah Jesus will be. They can't understand this until after the Resurrection. But Jesus wants people to accept his full identity, as a Messiah who must die, and not just come to him for healing, or entertainment, or free food.

We're lucky. We live on the other side of the most important event in the gospel story – the Resurrection. For the leper and the apostles in today's gospel, the resurrection hadn't happened yet. Even when Jesus told them it would happen, they didn't understand. But for us, it's not a secret. We know Jesus is alive, and is the Messiah, and is God incarnate, and we've been told to tell others – not to keep the secret any longer.

But, do we sometimes act as though the good news about Jesus is still a secret? We can do this in different ways. Maybe we believe everything the Church teaches about Jesus – that he is true God and true man. He was raised from the dead. He is coming again in glory. He is present in the Eucharist we celebrate here. But when we leave Church, do we keep these things to ourselves? If someone asks us about him, do we get a little embarrassed? Maybe we act as though there's a secret when we shouldn't.

Or, maybe we don't hesitate to tell others we believe in Jesus, that we're Christians. But maybe the Jesus we believe in, and tell others about, is a Jesus we've created in our own image. We see him as a helper, or a friend, or a source of good stories – but not as God, not as Lord of our lives. Maybe we pick and choose parts of the truth about Jesus that we like but ignore the parts that make us uncomfortable. Maybe the secret is that we have our own idea about who we think Jesus is, and that's what we worship.

Secrets. There's a time to keep a secret, and a time to tell a secret. And if we're keeping the real identity of Jesus a secret – then it's time to tell the secret.

There's an irony in today's gospel: when Jesus heals the leper, the leper is free to enter society, which he had been forbidden to do. But since the leper doesn't keep secret what Jesus did for him, Jesus can no longer enter the towns freely. In a sense, Jesus has taken the leper's place. And in a sense, Jesus has taken our place as well. He died for our sins, but it's no secret that he was also raised from the dead. The Church has proclaimed this since the first Easter Sunday, and we've been told to share it, not to keep it a secret. But – do we?

In the end, we're a lot like the hobbits. We're being led through the wilderness, sometimes hungry and thirsty, sometimes not exactly sure where we're headed. At the end of our story, we're also looking forward to the Return of the King. But there's no secret about who our king is: it's Jesus. And we should not try to keep what he has done for us, what he is doing for us, a secret.

HOW TO BE A LIGHT
Matthew 5:14

Tuesday of the Tenth Week in Ordinary Time, 9 June 2015

Jesus said to his disciples, "You are the light of the world." We're his disciples, so that means us. You, me, we're the light of the world. Do you feel like the light of the world? or do you feel more like you need a little light?

Many of us would probably say we've felt both ways. As friends, as parents, in many situations in our lives, we try to do good; we try to be light for the world. But at times, most of us have probably wished we could shine a little brighter than we do. Even when we feel like that – Jesus says, "you are the light of the world."

This gospel comes from the Sermon on the Mount, and the image of light Jesus used is found in the Hebrew Scriptures, our Old Testament. Today's psalm is a helpful example; it says, "(t)he revelation of your words sheds light... Lord, let your face shine on me." This reminds us that although we are the light of the world, we're not the ultimate source of light. People see what we do, but the first and greatest source of light is God. Jesus told his disciples that they were the light of the world – because they were his disciples.

Light bulbs don't make the electricity that makes them shine. Oil lamps don't make the oil they burn. And we don't make the light we shine with. It's the light of Jesus. Our prayer, and our participation in the Eucharist and other sacraments, help us keep our lights burning brightly. And the answers to prayer, and the grace we receive in the sacraments, come from God.

God knows, the world we live in needs that light. Last night, Tanya and I attended a class that's required for us to qualify as foster parents, and we listened to statistics on how many thousands of children have to be placed in foster care each year, just in Virginia, because of various forms of abuse. Our world needs light. But so did the world those first disciples lived in. And Jesus knows us, as he knew them. So when we feel a bit dimmer than we should, we shouldn't despair; Jesus can recharge us.

We are the light of the world, and we can keep shining into dark places, as long as we shine with the light of Christ.

GETTING WHAT WE NEED
1 Kings 17:7-16

Tuesday of the Tenth Week in Ordinary Time, 7 June 2016

The Rolling Stones have a well-known song… "You Can't Always Get What You Want…."[9] Today's first reading tells a story about people getting what they need, which was enough food to stay alive during a famine.

These people were a widow, and her son, and the prophet Elijah. They got the food they needed by what we might call a miracle, or maybe better, a series of daily miracles. The widow had enough food for one more meal when Elijah came along. But because she followed his instructions, which really came from God, her flour and oil lasted for a year, and they didn't starve to death. Every day when the widow went to get more flour – it was there. Another small but significant daily miracle.

On the other hand, as far as we know, flour and oil were it. Flour and oil, to make bread. Every day. Bread. Every day. Day after day. For months. Nothing to eat but bread. Maybe not what they wanted, even if it was what they needed. This is one of the interesting things about miracles in the Bible. When one of the prophets or Jesus perform a miracle, people often get what they need – but just what they need – and not a lot more.

God could give us anything we want. But he doesn't. You can't always get what you want. God could make us smart and rich and beautiful. He could give us a feast every day. But he doesn't. God knows what's best for us, and often what's best for us is getting what we need, but maybe not what we want.

Old Testament stories often prefigure New Testament stories. There are obvious connections between stories about Elijah and stories about Jesus, for example. When Jesus began healing people and feeding them miraculously, a lot of people thought maybe he was a prophet like Elijah, or maybe even Elijah himself come back to life. Jesus was actually much more than that. But Elijah's miracles and the miracles of Jesus have the same source – the power of God – and they have other things in common as well. Including this idea of getting what we need.

So it shouldn't surprise us that the Church Jesus founded works the same way. It shouldn't surprise us that the Eucharist, the bread that becomes the

---

[9] Homily text modified slightly here to avoid quoting lyrics.

body of Jesus, which is also prefigured in these stories, works the same way. It doesn't prevent us from making mistakes. It doesn't make us smart and beautiful. It doesn't prevent us from ever getting hungry again. But it does give us what we need – God's grace – for our everyday lives.

So it's true, we can't always get what we want. But, when we pray and read the scriptures and receive communion, we just might find we get what we need.

BAD THINGS, GOOD PEOPLE
Matthew 5:45

Tuesday of the Eleventh Week in Ordinary Time, 16 June 2015

When I was in high school, there was a best-selling book called *When Bad Things Happen to Good People*.[10] Someone gave my father a copy, and I remember seeing it in his study and thinking, "that's a good question. Why do bad things happen to good people?"

This wasn't long before I went to college and decided to major in philosophy and religion, and I soon realized that this was one of the big questions, one that wouldn't go away. Why do bad things happen to good people? Or, to turn it around, why do good things happen to bad people? In the words of today's gospel, why does God make "his sun rise on the bad and the good, and... rain to fall on the just and the unjust?" This question ranks right up there with "does God exist?" Actually, the two questions are related. If there is a good, all-knowing, all-powerful God, why do bad people get away with so much bad stuff? and why do bad things happen to good people?

I'm not going to try to answer those questions right now. I just want to point out that God knows we ask these questions; God even seems to encourage them. The words I quoted from the gospel are the words of Jesus. He's affirming that this is the way of the world. Sometimes bad things do happen to good people, while good things happen to bad people. Jesus does not avoid or deny this reality. Instead, he tells us to love our enemies, not hate them.

After all, if ever there was a good person, it was Jesus, and with him, his mother. And if ever something bad happened to good people, it was when Jesus was betrayed and crucified, while Mary watched. Yet Jesus forgave his killers.

Why does God let his people suffer? Especially innocent people, such as children? Sometimes someone tries to answer this question after some terrible thing has happened, and their answers insult or upset those who are suffering. I don't want to do that. I just hope we can remember that Jesus knows these things happen. He knows because he survived terrible things himself. He knows when we suffer. He knows we're asking "Why, God?" and

---

[10] *When Bad Things Happen to Good People*, Reprint Edition, Harold S. Kushner, 2004, Anchor. 176 pages.

"How, God?" And he's not avoiding the questions, even when we can't find the answers.

PATIENCE AND AHAB
1 Kings 21:17-29

Tuesday of the Eleventh Week in Ordinary Time, 14 June 2016

We just heard part of the story of King Ahab and his queen Jezebel. They had conspired to have a man named Naboth killed so Ahab could take his vineyard. So Ahab was a murderer and a thief, and we also know that Jezebel had persuaded him to ignore God and worship idols. But despite these things, when Ahab listened to the prophet Elijah and repented, God delayed his punishment. And this is just one of many examples in the Bible of God's mercy.

We're living in the Jubilee Year of Mercy proclaimed by Pope Francis.[11] The Pope has asked us to recognize this year of mercy by doing acts of mercy ourselves, and for me at least, that's easier to do when I'm reminded that God is much more merciful towards us than we could ever be towards one another.

I've been hearing stories of Ahab and Jezebel since I was a kid. When I hear about them, I pretty quickly categorize them in my mind – as evil, as ungodly, as sinners. Because they were, right? They were murderers, and thieves, and idolaters. They were obviously sinners – not just everyday sinners like we all are, but big-time sinners. But despite this God showed Ahab mercy when he repented. God was patient with Ahab rather than immediately punishing him. And when I hear this story, I think it can help me adjust my attitude at least a little bit in the right direction, towards showing mercy even to people who seem to be the obvious bad guys in our lives and our society.

What that means, exactly, we have to decide on a case-by-case basis, on a day-by-day basis. But surely patience is one of the virtues we need to develop, and bearing wrongs patiently is one of the spiritual works of mercy recognized by the Church. And dealing with the Ahabs and Jezebels in our lives – or even with folks who aren't nearly that bad – will help us develop patience.

When I was writing this homily about patience, I got a phone call that did exactly this – tested my patience. I was trying to write, and I was hoping to get finished quickly, and I really wanted the conversation to last less than the

---

[11] 8 December 2015 to 20 November 2016, formally proclaimed in the papal document *Misericordiae Vultus*.

21 minutes that it did last. (Yes, I timed it.) Be careful what you ask for; be careful what you preach about.

Of course tedious phone calls are nothing like killing someone so you can steal their vineyard, which is what Ahab did to Naboth. But if I can't be patient with a long-winded person on the phone, I don't know if I'll do well if I ever have to deal with an Ahab or a Jezebel.

I hope you're all more patient that I am. But regardless of who or what tests our patience, I hope that our reception of the body and blood of Jesus will help us all be more aware of God's mercy in our lives, and more ready to show mercy to the others we meet.

FATHERS AND FREEDOM
Galatians 3:26-29

Twelfth Sunday in Ordinary Time (Father's Day), 19 June 2016

The past month or so has been graduation season, the time of year when students finish their work at high schools and colleges and other schools, and celebrate their accomplishments, and move on to a new phase of their lives. Since the middle of May I've been to a community college graduation, and a home school graduation, and then last Friday, I went to a graduation that was different from any other I'd ever seen. It was a graduation at a prison.

Some of you know that last semester I taught a class at a prison in Lunenburg County.[12] I've been teaching for about 20 years, but that was something new for me as a teacher. As you can imagine, teaching in the prison was different in many ways from teaching regular college classes, and so was the graduation.

In some ways it was the same: we were wearing caps and gowns, we gave out diplomas, and there was lots of clapping and cheering for the graduates. But to get in, I had to have my name on an approved visitors list, I went through a metal detector, my shoes went through the X-ray machine, and I was patted down. We were all behind barbed wire fences, there were armed guards standing all around the room where the ceremony took place, and all of the graduates were prisoners.

Some of the prisoners had family members there who had come to see them graduate, and several children were there. It was obvious once the ceremony was over that the opportunity to visit with their family members was something else that made this a special day for the graduates.

Some researchers have suggested that there's a connection between a father's role in a family and his children's chances of committing a crime or being imprisoned. People argue about the conclusions that can be reached from such research. But no one seems to have data that show that having less influence from a good father is a positive thing. And common sense, as well as our faith, should tell us that having fathers involved with raising their children should be good – not just in terms of keeping them out of jail, but in lots of other ways as well.

---

[12] Lunenburg Correctional Center, just outside the town of Victoria in Lunenburg County, Virginia.

With that in mind, something I saw at the prison graduation stuck in my mind. After the ceremony ended, during the visiting time, one of the prisoners was sitting in a folding chair, earnestly talking to his two little children, who were also sitting in chairs, looking at him. He was gesturing and talking intently, obviously excited to see them, and trying to get as much as he could out of the short time, he had to visit with them.

It made me wonder what the impact of this father was in his children's lives. It made me wonder whether, in his childhood, his own father had ever talked to him like that. Was he an example of that possible correlation between lack of input from a father and increased chance of going to jail? Or maybe his own father had also been a prisoner at some time? Maybe his father was a great guy. Or maybe not. And of course at some level, when someone does something wrong, they usually bear some personal responsibility as well. And plenty of people who have negative relationships with their parents still end up as decent people, and don't go to jail. In this man's case, I don't know – but I was thinking about all this as we approached Father's Day.

And thinking about things like this on Father's Day[13] might make any of us consider our own relationships with our fathers. All of us have earthly fathers, and no doubt we have had a wide variety of relationships with them, from very positive, to not so positive, to none at all. We all have different stories.

And speaking of fathers, here at Church, it won't be long before you hear God referred to as your father – in fact, we hear it every time we recite the creed, right? I believe in God, the Father almighty.... And today, our second reading from Galatians calls Christians children of God. So we say that we all have two fathers, an earthly one and a heavenly one. And we say that no matter what the nature of your relationship with your earthly father is, you were made to have a positive, loving, and eternal relationship with your heavenly father. That's all true.

But today's reading from Galatians also reminds us that we have another father. If you're a Christian, you're not only God's child, and the child of your earthly parents – you also are Abraham's children. And that gives you a certain privilege. If we're Abraham's children – if Abraham is our father – then Paul said "we're heirs according to the promise." That means we're all somehow in a position to inherit something from our father Abraham.

---

[13] I'm well aware that Father's Day is not a church holiday, but in this case I felt that fatherhood was a natural thing to address based on the readings we had, and considering that it was probably on people's minds anyway.

As children of Abraham, we have access to a special relationship with God – one in which he sends his Spirit to fill our lives. The book of Genesis tells us that God established a special relationship with Abraham and his descendants. He would be their God, and they would be his people. That referred first of all to the Hebrew people, and it still does.

But because of Jesus, now anyone can be adopted into the family of Abraham. And all of us who are part of that adopted family receive God's spirit – Paul explains this in chapter 4 of Galatians. This is why Pope Pius XI in September 1938 said "(t)hrough Christ and in Christ we are the spiritual descendants of Abraham," and then famously concluded his remarks with the statement, "Spiritually, we are Semites."[14]

So welcome to the family, of God, and of Abraham. If you're a baptized Christian, you are a member of the family of God, and the family of Abraham. And this has powerful implications about how we live our lives. As Christians it means that we shouldn't ignore the Old Testament in our liturgy and our study and our personal prayer and reading. And in the Church, we don't. It means we can feel a special bond – what we might call family ties – with the Jewish people. And it means that we have a point of contact with Muslims as well, since they consider Abraham a great prophet, and like us, an example of faith.

On the other hand, ignoring or rejecting God as our Father, and Abraham as our father, might be even more dangerous spiritually than being rejected by our earthly fathers. If having a broken relationship with an earthly father can make a man more likely to end up in prison, and cause other sorts of problems as well – what does having a broken relationship with our spiritual fathers mean?

Today is a good day for each of us to ask ourselves if we feel like a member of the family of Abraham, or if our relationship with God feels like a father/child relationship should feel. Our faith is not meant to be just an abstract set of philosophical principles, though it can inspire great philosophy. And it's not meant to be just a one-to-one relationship between you and God, though that one-to-one relationship is critically important. In a very important sense, being a Christian is being part of a family.

---

[14] Allocution to the Belgian Pilgrims, 16 September 1938, quoted and reaffirmed by Benedict XVI on 12 September 2008 in his meeting with representatives of the Jewish community in Paris, France. Both documents available at www.vatican.va.

God is our father, Abraham is our father, and as Catholics, we also have a Holy Father in Rome. On Father's Day, when we honor our earthly fathers, we're blessed also to be able to reach out to our heavenly father and ask him to help us strengthen all of these relationships. As Catholics, we're given the sacraments to help us do that – the Eucharist which we celebrate now, as well as the other sacraments, especially reconciliation, which is a comfort and a help when we've been disobedient children.

I don't know that prisoner at the prison graduation who I saw talking to his children – he wasn't one of my students. I don't know how long it might be before he's released and will have less restrictions on spending time with his children. But I know that for us, it's not God who keeps us from spending time with him, with our heavenly Father.

We might not be in prison physically, but many of us are locked in by bad habits. Many of us are fenced in by ways of thinking and acting that keep us from talking to our father as freely as we should. But as children of Abraham, and as children of God, we don't have to stay behind the prison walls that keep us from having the relationships we should have. Prayer, repentance, receiving the sacraments, and Jesus can set us free.

PEARLS BEFORE SWINE
Matthew 7:6

Tuesday of the Twelfth Week in Ordinary Time, 23 June 2015

Some of you might be familiar with a comic strip called *Pearls Before Swine*. It features a character named Pig, who is a pig, and who is rather naive, and often a source of humor. The comic has generated some mild controversy;[15] I don't think much of it is inspired by the Gospel of Matthew other than its title, which comes from Matthew 7:6: "Do not give what is holy to dogs, or throw your pearls before swine...."

This verse is only found in Matthew, in the Sermon on the Mount. It might have already been a proverb when Jesus used it, and the image, casting pearls before swine, is well-known today, even if people don't always remember where it came from. I've heard this phrase used many times when one group of people refuses to listen to another, or is unable to listen to them, and someone says, "don't waste your time – don't cast your pearls before swine." Maybe such casual use of Jesus' words in comics and casual conversations dilutes the impact of this saying for us.

By the second century, the early Church applied this verse to the Eucharist: in the Didache, one of the earliest Christian writings outside the New Testament, this verse is quoted when Christians are warned that only baptized believers should be allowed to participate in the Eucharist.[16]

Certainly the Eucharist is one of our treasures that we should respect and safeguard. But the verse seems to apply to anything that is truly holy. In Matthew's text, this verse comes immediately after Jesus warns someone to remove the beam (or log) from their own eye before they judge someone else who only has a splinter in their eye. Reading these passages together suggests that we're called to look closely at what we consider holy before we judge others.

---

[15] For example, because of the character Rat's negative attitudes towards Christianity and the strip's insulting attitude towards some other comics.

[16] This is the last sentence of chapter 9 from the translation by M. B. Riddle in *Ante-Nicene Fathers*, Vol. 7, 1886, Buffalo: "But let no one eat or drink of your Thanksgiving (Eucharist), but they who have been baptized into the name of the Lord; for concerning this also the Lord has said, Give not that which is holy to the dogs."

So, we need to be sure we know what a pearl really is. We need to know what is truly holy. We don't want to throw pearls to pigs, intentionally or accidentally. Do we recognize what is holy, and treat the right things as holy? Do we ever toss what is holy to the pigs? Jesus and his Church will guide us, so we do see clearly when we answer these questions.

IN THE BOAT WITH JESUS
Matthew 8:23

Tuesday of the Thirteenth Week in Ordinary Time, 30 Jun 2015

Jesus got into a boat, his disciples followed him. This has been an image of the Church since its earliest days: the Church as a boat, and Jesus in the boat with us.

A boat can be many things. Transportation, from one side of the sea to the other. A means to make a living, if you're a fisherman, or a ferryman. Shelter, if you're caught in a storm, or you decide to live on a houseboat.

Imagine us in the place of the disciples, in the boat with Jesus. He got into the boat first. He led the way, and we should follow, if we don't want to be left on the wrong side of the sea. And for us, the boat is not just transportation. The disciples' ride in the boat was frightening. A storm came and tested their trust and their understanding of who Jesus was. The storm was violent enough that the disciples thought they might die.

So here we are, in the boat with Jesus, and storms are rocking the boat. Our Supreme Court has just ruled that same-sex marriages are legal in our nation. And even though the court majority was as small as it could be, and even though no court can change the definition of the sacrament of marriage, which is given by God, not humans, many people are applauding the court, while ignoring God. The boat is rocking. This same court, though with different members, ruled in 1973 that killing innocent, unborn children is legal in our nation, and since then has refused on many occasions to admit how wrong that ruling is. In some ways our boat has been rocking since 1973; it's been a long and violent storm.

But in some ways, our boat is always rocking. Sin is always present, in one form or another. The Church has always had her enemies. And our place has always been in the boat with Jesus. During the storm, the disciples awoke Jesus. That's an image of prayer – not political activism. And the disciples were amazed at what Jesus did when he woke up.

So we should pray, and not think that prayer is a mild or ineffective response to the storm. Eventually, Jesus will calm the storm, even if we can't imagine when, and are amazed at how He does it. Eventually, the boat will reach the other side of the sea, and we'll climb out, and the weather will be beautiful.

THE WINEBERRIES ARE RIPE
Matthew 9:37-38

Tuesday of the Fourteenth Week in Ordinary Time, 7 July 2015

When I was 16 my family moved to a new house on a dead-end gravel road in the country. One thing we liked about our new home was that all around it, on the sides of the road, beside the creeks, at the edges of the forest, grew wineberry vines. Wineberries[17] are a type of raspberries, but have their own slightly different taste. The thorns on their vines aren't as strong as the ones on blackberries, and when they're ripe, they're easy to pick. And they're delicious.

Several years after we moved, all the roads in our county got new names, and our road was named Wineberry Lane. My Dad still lives on Wineberry Lane, and when we went to see him last weekend, on the fourth of July, the wineberries were ripe. So before we left, Jeremy and Anna went out and picked a few pounds of wineberries, which Jeremy and Luisa later turned into wineberry jelly. Which is also delicious.

There are so many ripe wineberries on Wineberry Lane right now that if you sent out a dozen people, they could pick berries all day and still not get them all. "The harvest is abundant, but the laborers are few." Right now, that's true if you're talking about wineberries; it's also true if you're talking about the Church.

Our Church is under attack. The truths that we proclaim are being denied, and this might make us feel that it's time to defend ourselves. But this also shows us how many people out there could be added to the Church. It might be hard to see, but a lot of these people are ripe for the picking, or soon will be. If we only focus on our sense of being attacked, we might forget how many people need to hear the truth from us in a positive way.

In the gospel, Jesus tells his disciples to pray for workers. He doesn't say to fight and destroy people who disagreed with him, even though they were there, accusing him of working with demons. He said his followers should pray for workers who would help with the harvest. Yes, we should defend the truth – the truth about families, the truth about marriage and the other sacraments, the truth about the value of every human life, and other truths.

---

[17] Also known as wine raspberries, dewberries, or *Rubus phoenicolasius* to botanists.

But being defensive is not what the Church is all about. It's also about harvesting.

Right now it's wineberry harvest time. But in a month, the wineberries will be gone until next year. And right now, it's also harvest time for some of the people around us. Christians before us have prayed that God would send workers – and he did. Us. So what are we doing to help with the harvest?

We call this work evangelism, and we're all called to make it part of our lives. Don't just take my word for it – here's what Pope Francis says: "Every Christian is challenged, here and now, to be actively engaged in evangelization; indeed, anyone who has truly experienced God's saving love does not need much time or lengthy training to go out and proclaim that love."[18] And how do we do that? "...the first step is personal dialogue, when the other person speaks and shares his or her joys, hopes and concerns for loved ones, or so many other heartfelt needs. Only afterwards is it possible to bring up God's word...."[19]

We can all do this. Talk to others, and let them know we care about them, whoever they are, and whatever they think of us. And we shouldn't be surprised when we find the fruit is ripe, because that's what Jesus told us to expect.

---

[18] *Evangelii Gaudium*, section 120.
[19] *Evangelii Gaudium*, section 128.

GOOD WORKERS NEEDED
Matthew 9:37-38

Tuesday of the Fourteenth Week in Ordinary Time, 5 Jul 2016

Today's gospel from Matthew repeats something we heard on Sunday from Luke.[20] Jesus tells his followers, "ask the master of the harvest to send out laborers for his harvest."

What happens to a crop if it isn't harvested? If Leslie and George[21] left their grapes on the vine and never picked them, they would split and wrinkle and shrivel, and they'd get no wine, right? And what happens to grain if it isn't harvested? The seeds fall to the ground, no bread gets made from that grain, and it feeds no one.

The harvest Jesus saw was people with all kinds of needs, both physical and spiritual. Like the people we live with today. Today's gospel, like the entire gospel story, tells us that Jesus healed people who were sick and fed people who were hungry, as well as meeting their spiritual needs by teaching and preaching.

One of the messages we often hear from the Church, because the apostles learned it from Jesus, is that we're called to help people. But in today's gospel, and in Sunday's gospel, there's also a clear statement that we need to pray that God will send others to help them as well. Jesus saw the needy people around him as a harvest that needs to be harvested. But he didn't tell everyone to go immediately and start picking the grapes or grain. He told them to pray for the right people to come and do the harvesting.

What would happen if just anyone went and started picking grapes whenever they felt like it? Grapes would get picked before they were ripe, or they would get picked too late, or the vines might be damaged. Not everyone knows what it takes to pick grapes – but not everyone needs to do that job.

Any one of us can only fill certain needs. We each have pretty specific abilities. And the Church is made of people like us. Not everyone is called to be a winemaker, or a foreign missionary, or a Dominican priest. But each of us is called to pray for the whole Church and for the harvest that needs to be gathered – for the people who need Jesus, and need our help, one way or another. We do that together here at Mass, and we can do it privately as well.

---

[20] Cf. Matthew 9:37-38 and Luke 10:1-2.
[21] A couple in our parish who own and operate Thistle Gate Vineyard near Scottsville, Virginia.

We're often concerned about our own individual vocation, our place in the big plan – what sort of harvesting we're supposed to do. But even while we're waiting for our exact role in the harvest to become clear, Jesus asks us to pray for the workers that are needed, here and everywhere in the world.

PUTTING THE SHEEP FIRST
Mark 6:34

Sixteenth Sunday in Ordinary Time, 19 July 2015

Last week Jeremy and I took a short trip to western North Carolina. We went there to climb Cold Mountain. You might have heard of a novel named for the mountain that won the National Book Award and was the basis for a movie. Although the book is fiction, the mountain is real, and it's over 6000 feet tall, one of the highest in the eastern United States.

The route that Jeremy and I took to the top of Cold Mountain and back was more than 10 miles long, and I was surprised by how rocky the trail was. I moved more slowly than I thought I would, and Jeremy waited patiently for me. By the time we got back to the car we were mostly talking about two things: how tired we were, and what we were going to get for supper.

Some of you have had similar experiences. Maybe you've climbed a mountain, or been coming home from a long trip, or worked much later than normal, or been outside in bad weather all day, or spent hours or days sitting by the bed of a sick family member. Maybe lunch time came and went with no lunch, and you weren't sure about supper.

Jesus and the apostles were in a situation like that. Jesus had sent the apostles out to preach. He told them not to take food or money or extra clothes with them. Now they'd come back to tell Jesus what had happened, and they'd been so busy they hadn't had a chance to eat. So they all got in a boat and went to find food and a place to rest.

But when they got where they were going, more people were there, waiting for them. The gospel says these people were like sheep without a shepherd, and Jesus felt pity and started to teach them. Despite being tired and hungry himself, Jesus recognized their needs. They were like sheep, and Jesus made himself their shepherd. We sometimes say that Jesus is the good shepherd, and here we see what that means in practical terms. It means putting the sheep's needs ahead of his own; it means putting the sheep first. And that can be hard.

When I got down from Cold Mountain the other day, I was not in the mood to fix someone else dinner or teach a class. I was not in the mood to do much else except what we did – find a Mexican restaurant, eat, ride around a little bit, then go crash at our hotel. If we heard that Jesus and the apostles went away to a quiet place and had dinner, and then spent some time resting before returning to their teaching and healing ministry, it wouldn't seem surprising. Why shouldn't they?

Some of you can remember when a certain fast food chain used this rhyme in its ads: "You deserve a break today, so get up and get away...." Jesus was human; he got tired and hungry. He deserved a break that day. But that's not what he got. Because for Jesus, the sheep came first.

His actions were an example for the apostles. They remembered this story, and it became part of the gospels. In the next part of the story, the apostles ask Jesus what to do so all the people with them can eat, and this leads to the Feeding of the 5000 – a story that's about physical as well as spiritual food. A little preview of coming attractions: this is the background for our gospels for the next five Sundays: the good shepherd feeding his sheep.

Jesus became a shepherd to people who reminded him of sheep, and he put them first. He gave them physical food, and then he left them the Eucharist. And Jesus is our shepherd as well. Psalm 100 says "we are his people, the sheep of his pasture." He put us first by dying for us, and by giving his body to feed us during our lives as Christians. Jesus feeds us through the Eucharist, and He teaches us through the Church.

So we're like the people who Jesus saw as sheep. But, we're also like the apostles in this story. And like the apostles in the early Church, sometimes we also have to take the role of the shepherd. As Christians, Jesus is our model as well as our shepherd. And that means that sometimes in our lives we'll have to put the sheep first. And who are they? Who do you know who needs help?

In John chapter 10, Jesus says that his sheep know his voice, and he knows them. So if we're going to be like Jesus, we'll know our sheep, and we'll put our sheep first. We know it's possible. Think of someone who has been an example of sacrificial love in your life, someone who put your needs ahead of their own. Parents, spouses, or friends often do this, whether just out of human kindness, or because they're consciously imitating Jesus. Saints are also well known for this kind of behavior, so we have examples. And we know where the strength to do this comes from. Jesus is our shepherd and he feeds us; that gives us strength to feed others. Being a sheep gives strength when it's time to be a shepherd.

Sometimes we are like hungry sheep. When we've been traveling and working, and it's time to get up and get away, we need to do that to stay healthy. It's part of being human. Physically, we need food and rest; spiritually, we need to be here, at Mass. But sometimes we need to act like shepherds, and when we do, Jesus is our model. We need to get to know the sheep he sends us, and we need to put those sheep first, like Jesus did, even if it means going hungry ourselves for a little longer.

RECOGNIZING THE TRINITY
Genesis 18:1-10

Sixteenth Sunday in Ordinary Time, 17 July 2016

It was July 2009. I'd been in Italy, and I'd just boarded the plane at the Rome airport that was going to bring me back home. The plane was full, and a lot of excited young people, mostly college-aged, were talking and moving around on the plane as we waited to take off. I'd already found my seat when another passenger asked me if I would switch seats with them. I didn't mind, so I moved up a few seats, and found myself sitting beside a young woman who was quietly looking out the window.

At first, she didn't say anything, but eventually, after the plane took off, we started to talk a little. She told me her name was Ariana, and she said she that was very tired. I asked why, and she said that she was on her way home from a swim meet. I remembered that a few days before at a hotel, I'd seen part of a TV broadcast of a swim meet in Rome, and I'd watched long enough to realize that it was the world championships.

And then I suddenly realized who all the healthy-looking, excited young men and women on this plane were – they were the U.S. swim team. So I asked Ariana, "what event did you swim in?" and she said, "the 200 IM." And I said, "Oh. Do you mind me asking how you did?" And she said very quietly, "I won." And then she paused slightly, and then said, "I set a world record."

So here I was with my backpack full of dirty laundry sitting beside a world-record-setting swimmer. But she just looked like a nice, normal, college student, like someone who might show up in one of my classes. In fact, a little later we talked about the classes she had been taking the previous school year. It was an interesting conversation for several reasons, and one of them was that Ariana seemed so normal, yet she was an extraordinary person, even though I didn't recognize that at all when I first saw her.

I remembered meeting her when I read our first reading from Genesis earlier this week. It tells a story about Abraham meeting someone exceptional – three someones, in fact. But I'm no Abraham – and although I didn't recognize a great swimmer when I saw one, Abraham knew he was dealing with someone important when he saw three men, and he reacted quickly when they appeared.

But what do we think when we hear this story? Do we recognize the significance of these three men? If we don't listen carefully, and if we don't know what this story has meant to the Church down through the years, we might miss something. Some things we're not told directly. We don't know the names of these men, or what they looked like, and we aren't told where they came from. But Abraham treats them as if they're extraordinary, and at the end of the story, one of them says something that is extraordinary.

Like a lot of Bible stories, this one has been shown in many paintings, and it has been the inspiration for icons that have been used by Christians for many centuries in their prayer. But when this scene is painted, or an icon of this scene is made, it's not usually called an image of Abraham's Three Visitors or something like that. Instead, it's called an icon of the Trinity. But how can a picture of these three men be a picture of the Trinity?

According to the Church, the Trinity is a mystery — something that can't be completely explained, something that will always be partly beyond explanation. But that doesn't mean we don't talk about it, or shouldn't talk about it — instead, it means we will always be able to talk about it. We'll never run out of things to say or think about the Trinity. And for centuries, Christian art and iconography has helped us do that.

One of the best-known icons in Christian history was made by the Russian painter Andrei Rublev. It's called Rublev's *Icon of the Trinity*, and it shows the three men from this story sitting around a table, with food on the table, looking at one another. If you look closely, you can see that they have wings, which makes it seem that they're angels. And if we remember that an angel is essentially a messenger from God, that makes sense, because they do deliver a message: that Sarah will have a son — even though she was infertile.

I have a copy of this icon here today, and you can take a look at it after Mass if you're not familiar with it. But why is it considered a picture of the Trinity, and not the three angels, or something like that? If we look more closely at the story, we can see why. It begins by saying that "(t)he Lord appeared to Abraham," but then tells a story of three men appearing. Abraham immediately bowed down to these men without asking who they were.

If there were three men, why did Abraham refer to them as "Sir" in the singular? and if they were angels, why didn't they tell Abraham not to worship them, like angels do in other Biblical stories? How long did it take to prepare them a meal, since the servants had to kill and prepare a steer, and why were these men willing to wait patiently? And how did the man or men know Sarah's name, if Abraham had not told them?

Well, to answer the last question first – God knows everything, so he would not only know Sarah's name, he would also know that in a year she would have a son – and she did. And God would know that Abraham had been wondering how, or maybe even if, God would keep his promise to give him many descendants.

As for the patience of these three men, God knows how to be perfectly patient with us when he's waiting for us to serve him, like Abraham served these men, including times when he's waiting on us to recognize him in our everyday lives. And Abraham gave these men something valuable – a whole steer – just as God asks us to give generously to him.

And this is also a clue: there are three men, but we hear only one voice, and only one will is expressed. This is consistent with our understanding of the Trinity: three persons, but one God, who does not contradict himself, and who is consistent in what he says, whether he speaks to us as Father, Son, or Holy Spirit.

Much more can be said about this story, and the images it has inspired, than I have time for today. But for now, consider this: for most people it's easier to remember stories than to remember long theological arguments. You can remember stories about things that happened to you, like when you meet someone remarkable on a plane, and you can remember stories people tell you. And anyone who can see can look at a picture, but not everyone can read and understand complicated theology. Biblical stories and pictures present theological truth in a way that simple statements don't, in a way that we can remember.

One story or image can contain layers of truth. And although this story about Abraham is a story about God fulfilling his promises, it's also something else – it contains more hints about the nature of God. So a picture of three men can also be a picture of three angels, and also, in a way, a picture of the Trinity.

Abraham recognized that the three men in the story deserved honor and sacrifice. This story can be an example of what our response to God should be – a God who is three persons. We should honor him, offer him sacrifices, and listen to what he has to tell us. But to do that, first we have to recognize him when he enters our lives.

I told you about not recognizing a great swimmer even though I was sitting next to her on the airplane. When I got home, I looked up news stories about the swim meet and read more details about her career. And she was telling me the truth about who she was. And later that year, this nice, quiet young lady I'd met on the plane was named an American Swimmer of the Year by *Swimming World* magazine[22] – and that was along with a guy named Michael Phelps, who was also on that plane, and who had also just set a world record at that swim meet.

Probably a lot of you have stories in your own life about seeing someone you knew and not recognizing them, or about someone seeing you and not recognizing you. As Christians, what we really don't want is to go through life not recognizing God when he walks into our lives, perhaps disguised as an ordinary person, or three.

We know Jesus is present in the Eucharist; as Catholics we recognize him there. We know that God created the world we live in and created us to live in this world. And we know the Holy Spirit meets us in the sacraments and comes to live within us. But when we're at home, in the middle of an ordinary day, like Abraham sitting in the entrance of his tent – do we recognize God then? Because God – Father, Son, and Holy Spirit – can come walking into our lives wherever we are, any time at all. And our prayer should be that we will recognize him and be ready for whatever surprising message he might have for us.

---

[22] More information about the winners is available at https://www.swimmingworldmagazine.com/news/swimming-world-names-2009-american-swimmers-of-the-year/

STRETCHING OUT HIS HAND
Exodus 14:21-27, 15:12; Matthew 12:49

Tuesday of the Sixteenth Week in Ordinary Time, 21 July 2015

> • Moses stretched out his hand over the sea....
> • ...the LORD told Moses, "Stretch out your hand over the sea...."
> • So Moses stretched out his hand over the sea....
> • When you stretched out your right hand, the earth swallowed them!
> • ...stretching out his hand toward his disciples, [Jesus] said, "Here are my mother and my brothers."[23]

The Red Sea parted, and the Hebrew people escaped the Egyptian army, when Moses stretched out his hand. But the psalm gives credit to God for stretching out His hand – God's hand – to save His people. The hand of Moses effectively became the hand of God.

The Israelites were concerned about their identity. Would they be slaves, or free people? And Jesus was concerned about identity. Who would recognize him for who he was? Who would be in his family? Our identity as Christians is confirmed at baptism, and the blessing of water in the Rite of Baptism says, "through the waters of the Red Sea you led Israel out of slavery, to be an image of God's holy people, set free from sin by baptism." And as the blessing continues, the minister reaches out his right hand to touch the water.

When we greet someone, we often extend our hand to shake. When we are talking and want to make a point, we might stick out our hand and shake our finger. When Superman wants to fly, he puts his hands out in front of him. Extending your hand adds emphasis. God could have parted the Red Sea without having Moses stretch out his hand, but God knows the effect of gesture.

The Gospel of Matthew often emphasizes parallels between Jesus and Moses. An important one is when Jesus went up the mountain for the Sermon on the Mount – just as Moses went up Sinai to receive the law. The detail of Jesus extending his hand is smaller, small enough that we might overlook it

---

[23] All of these quotations came from the day's readings. Unusually, the psalm for the day was not from the Psalms, but from Exodus 15, the song of Moses and the Israelites after crossing the Red Sea and escaping the Egyptians.

– but the hand of Jesus, even more than that of Moses, was the hand of God. And when he pointed it at his disciples, claiming them as his family, he was also pointing it at us.

THE GOD WHO REMOVES GUILT
Micah 7:18

Tuesday of the Sixteenth Week in Ordinary Time, 19 July 2016

It's hard to say how many names and descriptions for God we have in the Bible and in Church tradition. Some are single words, like Lord, and some are phrases like Ancient of Days or King of Kings. Since God is infinitely great it makes sense that we need many names and phrases to describe him. Every one of them helps us focus on God's goodness in a different way.

In our first reading God is called the God who removes guilt. These verses are from the very end of the book of Micah, one of the Minor Prophets, which we only hear in the Mass readings a few days each year. Micah had a lot to say about God's judgment on sin, but the book ends with words of hope, including this description of God as the God who removes guilt.

Micah lived roughly 2700 years ago. His people, God's people, had rejected God over and over since they had escaped Egypt and gained independence. They had demanded a king when God said they shouldn't have one, they'd split into two nations, and they'd ignored the laws God gave them. Micah warned them their nation would be destroyed if they continued to follow the path they were on. But he also appealed to the nature of God as the God who removes guilt, pointing to the cure for their unhealthy state.

We can see parallels in our own lives. Individually, we need our own guilt removed, and when we receive the sacrament of reconciliation, we hear another Biblical name for God, the Father of mercies, that complements his description as the God who removes guilt. But we also need our guilt removed as a nation, like the people Micah was speaking to. Even though we're not chosen in a special way as Israel was, our nation is also demanding things from our rulers that we shouldn't have. Our nation is also ignoring the laws that God has given us.

As individuals, we can go to confession, and we can know the feeling of guilt removed. But it seems harder to know how to help our nation. We should be concerned, because we know God's people lost their independence, just as Micah predicted they would, and it's not impossible that the same thing can happen to us. But we also know that their God is our God, and whatever the answer is for our nation, it has to center on the God who removes guilt.

DOING THE IMPOSSIBLE
Judges 6:11-24a

Tuesday of the Twentieth Week in Ordinary Time, 18 Aug 2015

One phrase kept coming to mind as I thought about this homily: *Mission: Impossible*. You might know the Tom Cruise movies with that name, or the TV show from the 80s, or the one from the 60s and 70s, which was the source of the name. But I want to talk about something older, and more important, and more exciting, than those... even if there are no car crashes. There might be a chariot crash, though.

Gideon said he was the least significant man in the least significant family of his tribe, but God called him to save Israel. To Gideon, it sounded like God was asking him to do the impossible.

Jesus said that it would be easier for a camel to go through the eye of a needle than for a rich man to enter heaven. In other words, as the disciples said, it was impossible. Gideon was faced with an impossible mission; the disciples were faced with an impossible situation. But Gideon did lead Israel to freedom. And we know some rich men have ended up in heaven. The impossible happened. And not just then. Our Church is built on doing the impossible.

Listen to these impossible things:

- Israelites trapped between the Red Sea and the Egyptian army... escape through the water, while the army sinks and drowns (there's the chariot crash).
- A virgin... has a son.
- A man who's crucified, dead, and buried... returns to life.
- Bread and wine... become human flesh and blood.

Christianity is about doing and believing the impossible, or it's about nothing. Take away the impossible from Christianity, and you turn it into something else. In our faith, in our lives, God makes the impossible possible. The impossible becomes possible when it's God's will, and when a person whom God calls accepts the mission impossible. It's not that God makes anything we want to happen possible. But when it's God's will, what seems impossible to us can happen, and does happen.

- It was God's will for Israel to be set free from Egypt, and from Midian. And they were.
- It's God's will for everyone to know him and live with him... even the rich. And some do.
- It was God's will for a virgin to have a son and fulfill prophecy. And she did.
- It was God's will for that same son to die... and to come back to life. And he did.
- It's God's will that bread and wine become the flesh and blood of that same son. And they do, and in a few moments, they will.

As we hear these truths from Holy Scripture and from our Church, and as we receive that same body and blood, we might consider this: what mission does God have for us – even if it seems impossible?

NO COSTUME IS GOOD ENOUGH
Ezekiel 28:2

Tuesday of the Twentieth Week in Ordinary Time, 16 Aug 2016

When I was in college, we had an annual event called the Beaux Arts Ball. It was a dance, but it was unusual because everyone went in costume, and the more outrageous the costume, the better. Someone dressed in a full gorilla suit, or dressed as Santa Claus, for example, would be pretty ordinary at this dance.

One year my roommate Brian and I decided to go, and I'm still not sure what I was dressed as, but my costume involved red plastic pants, the netting from a hammock, a bunch of plastic lizards, and black and white face paint. Not long after we arrived, a friend of ours walked up to us and said, "Hi Brian! Where's Mike?" I was so happy! I was standing right in front of her, and she didn't recognize me at all. My costume was a success.

Wearing a costume can be fun. But there's someone we can't fool no matter how good our costume is – and of course, that's God. It would be silly to think that you could wear a disguise to trick God. Even my Beaux Arts Ball costume was not that good.

But suppose you were so confused that you thought you could fool God. Suppose you were so confused that you thought you were someone else. Suppose you even thought you were a god, and you wanted other people to treat you that way That might sound like a definition of insanity, but in today's first reading we heard about someone like that.

Apparently, the Prince of Tyre had an identity problem. God told the prophet Ezekiel to tell him, "you are a man, and not a god, however you may think yourself like a god." It's one thing if someone else doesn't recognize you. But if you're honestly confused yourself about who you are, you have a problem. And if you think you're a god, and not human, you really have a problem.

The simple fact is – we're not God. I know if I put it that way, you're likely to respond, "no joke! I'm not feeling very omnipotent today!" But do we ever act like we think we're God? Even within the limited spheres of influence that we have, maybe we do.

Sometimes this shows up in ethics, when people get the idea that something is right or wrong simply because they think it is, rather than deciding what's good with reference to the way the world was created, and the one who created it. This is a common idea these days, that right and wrong are what we say they are. But many of us here, I think, would say that we intend to follow the ethical teachings of the Church based on reason and natural law and revelation. So is there any other way that we confuse ourselves with God?

Perhaps there's a more subtle way that this applies for us, something that happens when we sense that God wants us to do something specific in our lives, or maybe not do something, and we gently resist. We pretend we don't hear what God is telling us.

We often have choices. Sometimes they're minor, like which pair of socks do I wear today? But sometimes they're more significant, like taking a certain job, or a class, or going on a trip, or something like that. And if we simply think, "hey it's my life, I can do what I want..." are we sometimes forgetting who's God? Are we forgetting that he can see through our disguise?

At that moment when we're trying to decide, the moment before we decide, when we still have time to pray – that's when it might be helpful for us to stop and remember who we are. Because God made us and loves us, he might have an opinion on whether we should do something or not.

So it's helpful for us to have this reminder from the prophets that God is God, and we're not, and that forgetting that can lead to trouble. And no costume that we could ever wear can change that.

COMMUNITY, COMMUNION, AND THE OLYMPICS
Luke 13:29

Twenty-first Sunday in Ordinary Time, 21 Aug 2016

I don't normally watch a lot of television, but for the past two weeks I've been watching almost every night. You might guess why: the Olympics. Part of what interests me is seeing the actual competitions, and who will win – if Michael Phelps or Usain Bolt will win a final gold medal, if Brazil will win gold in men's soccer, or if someone we'd never heard of two weeks ago will become a household name, like Tori Bowie.[24]

But I've also been wondering if some part of the appeal of the Olympics comes from something else, something besides the achievements of the athletes, and something you won't hear the announcers mention on TV. I wonder if another thing we like about the Olympics is that it gives us a hint of what heaven will be like.

Now I'm not at all naive about the flaws of the Olympics. I know that planning for the games has involved scandals, and the actual events have been marred by cheating, and lying, and violence – not just the Rio games, but many of the previous ones as well. And I realize that some people might not care about them and might just wish they'd go away. Well, they end today.

But I have wondered why the Olympics appeal to so many people, despite what we know about their flaws, even people who aren't normally interested in sports. And I think one reason is because when the Olympics brings so many people together from so many places around the world, it's a little sign, or hint, of what heaven will be like, and deep inside, everyone wants that, even if they don't admit it. It's part of who we are as humans: we're made for heaven, and we're made to look for signs of eternal life while we live this life.

In today's gospel, people asked Jesus who would be saved – who could make it into the kingdom of heaven. He didn't give them a guarantee that everyone, everywhere would be saved. But he also didn't say that only people of a certain race or nationality could be saved. What he said was that "people will

---

[24] Bowie is a track and field athlete from the United States who won gold, silver, and bronze medals at the 2016 Olympic Games, followed by two golds at the track and field World Championships in 2017.

come from the east and the west and from the north and the south and will recline at table in the kingdom of God."

When I read that passage last week I was immediately reminded of the opening ceremony of the Olympics: "...people will come from the east and the west and from the north and the south...." That sounds like the Parade of Nations, all the teams from nations all over the world that came to Rio marching into the stadium. If you watched the opening ceremony, you know that there were a lot of teams – 205 nations sent teams, in fact, plus the independent team and the refugee team.

We know that our Church has a place for everybody, from anywhere and everywhere around the world. But what else in our life does? Not much, but the Olympic Games come close. Where else in the world do, we see – even just on TV – citizens of over 200 nations gathered together peacefully for one purpose? In the Parade of Nations, traditional enemies marched together. Iran and Iraq were both there, along with Israel. Both North and South Korea sent teams; so did mainland China as well as Taiwan. Suddenly we were seeing cooperation and fellowship between them, instead of fighting, even if it's for a brief time.

We know heaven will be a place of peace, and people seek peace and want peace, even though it's often hard to find in this life. But living in community with others goes together with living in peace. As humans, we're made to enjoy community – not just our local community, but world-wide community, and eternal community.

All humans, everywhere, are made in the image of God, and are made for an eternal relationship with God. God is a trinity, involved in eternal self-communion. But that implies that we are also made for eternal communion, with God and with others. And that communion is for everyone, despite our differences in history and language and talents. So we're made for heaven, a place of eternal peaceful communion with God and other people from other backgrounds, not just the same as us – people who will come from the east and the west and from the north and the south and will recline at table in the kingdom of God.

I mentioned the Olympic refugee team earlier, and that team has received some media attention at these games.[25] The presence of that team is a

---

[25] Information about their history and who was on the team is at https://www.olympic.org/refugee-olympic-team

reminder that about 1 out of every 113 people in the world right now lives displaced from their homeland. That's less than one percent, you might say – but in terms of the world population, that's more than 65 million people. In other words, more than the population of France, or Italy, a group large enough to be the 21st largest nation in the world if they were a separate nation.

These people have been forced from their homes by war, by famine, by disease, by religious persecution – things that we recognize as wrong. They represent weaknesses and imperfections in our attempts to live in community. And they represent a failure of our present lives to serve as a model for what eternal life should be like.

If we're meant to live forever in community in heaven, it makes sense that we'd try to start living that way here and now. The Church tries to do that, but our efforts have been flawed. The presence of so many refugees is evidence that we still have a long way to go, but the Church's response to these refugees, our concern for them, is evidence that we believe what we say when we say we believe in communion. And maybe including them in the Olympics is a hint of a broader human desire for that communion as well.

Of course the Olympics are not a perfect model of heaven, just a hint, as I said. It's very hard to qualify as an athlete in the Olympics, especially in a large country like ours. All those hundreds of athletes marching in the Parade of Nations were only a tiny fraction of all the athletes in the world, much less of all the people in the nations they represent. They are the elite. And that's something that's different about heaven. Jesus has made the way to heaven open for anyone, not just the elite. We don't have to be the fastest person to memorize the *Catechism* to get on the team, or even the second or third fastest person. We don't have to set a record for going to Mass more times than anyone else – not that going to Mass is bad, of course – but it's not a numbers game, and it's not a race.

I don't want to say that getting to heaven is easy. In today's gospel Jesus said "many... will attempt to enter but will not be strong enough." But we've been given the Church and the sacraments, and we're told that they're meant for anyone who wants to receive them. And we know that Jesus said that many people will come from the east and the west and from the north and the south and receive what he's given us.

The Olympics is not the only hint of heaven that we have. What we're doing here today is a little preview of our future, too. Every Mass looks towards our future in heaven, even as it also makes present the past, the crucifixion.

The Olympics can't do that. But by bringing so many people together in one place, even for a brief time, the Olympics can hint that this is the way it should be – that we should be looking for things in this life that point towards an eternal way of life that will involve people from every nation.

In a few hours, the Olympics will be over. It's hard to say how much good will be done by the sense of community they've tried to create. But after the Olympic Games are long gone, the Church will still be here. We'll still come together from every direction to worship in community, and to receive communion – to receive Jesus, the communion who makes communion possible. And our coming together here today and at every Mass shows our hope that we will one day all be together as part of a much larger group of people who have come from the east and the west and from the north and the south to recline at table in the kingdom of God.

ALWAYS TIME TO PRAY
Luke 6:12

Tuesday of the Twenty-third Week in Ordinary Time, 6 Sept 2016

Suppose a whole bunch of people want something from you (and maybe that *is* what you feel like today). They want you to fix their problems, as soon as possible. Meanwhile, you've got problems of your own. Their problems are real, but so are yours. Doesn't sound like fun, does it? But we could say that was the situation Jesus was in in the gospel we just heard. In a relatively short time, he'd gained a reputation as a healer – and there were a lot of sick people in Galilee, and so they came looking for him, even from faraway places. Who can blame them?

But little did they know – Jesus also had something else on his mind. He had come to start something new and different – what we now call the Church. And to do that, he needed to choose the right people to leave behind in charge of the Church once he was gone – the people we now know as the apostles. Out of those hundreds and thousands of followers, he had to choose just 12 – just the right ones.

So what did he do? He spent all night praying. Before he faced all the sick people who needed healing, and before he chose the 12 apostles, he added something else to his to-do list: prayer. Not just a quick prayer, but a whole night of prayer. And Jesus did something similar at the end of his public ministry – just before he was crucified, he spent all night in the Garden of Gethsemane praying. And as we hear the gospels, we realize that many times, when Jesus was very busy, he stopped to take time to pray.

More than 20 years ago a Protestant pastor wrote a book titled *Too Busy Not to Pray*.[26] I never read the book, but the title has stuck with me. It's a catchy way of emphasizing this point: that no matter how busy he was, Jesus always took time to pray. And when he was very busy, it seems that he was also very sure to take extra time to pray.

The message for us is clear, isn't it? Are we busy? Take time to pray. Are we extra busy? Take extra time to pray.

---

[26] 1994, InterVarsity Press. The author was Bill Hybels, the founding pastor of Willow Creek Community Church, a large church in Illinois. Sadly, Hybels was accused of misconduct in early 2018 and resigned as pastor.

WE'RE ALL TEACHERS
Mark 9:31-32

Twenty-fifth Sunday in Ordinary Time
(Catechetical Sunday), 20 Sept 2015

I have a question for you: are you a teacher? If you answer that question any way other than yes, I hope to change your mind. Not because I want you to become a teacher, but because you are a teacher, even if you don't apply that label to yourself, and even if no one else calls you that.

Today is Catechetical Sunday, the day we recognize teachers, especially those who have agreed to lead the Christian formation classes at our parish. They've agreed to wear this label, teacher, for us, and we're thanking them for that, and praying for them as the new school year begins. But what about everyone else?

Well, you came to Mass this morning – you're here. You chose to come here, and not go somewhere else. Maybe you wish you were somewhere else. Maybe you're hoping I won't preach too long because you're planning to go somewhere else soon. Well, I won't.

But we're all here because we identify ourselves as Christians, and our namesake, Jesus Christ – our savior, our guide, and our example – was a teacher. In the gospels, one of the things we see Jesus doing over and over is teaching. Both his enemies and his friends called him teacher. In today's gospel we hear this: "He was teaching his disciples... but they did not understand." If we follow Jesus, we need to be willing to teach, whether or not we wear the label teacher, and we need to be ready when we meet people who don't understand. And there are plenty of them out there.

If we're going to follow Jesus, then one way or another, we're called to teach. That might not mean teaching in a school, or in a parish. But by being here today, and not being somewhere else, you're already on the way to teaching our society something it needs to know. And our society is definitely confused about certain things.

It's been obvious lately that a lot of people in our society don't understand one basic idea that we share as Christians: the idea that every human being has dignity. This is a fundamental teaching of the Church, grounded on the statement in Genesis that every person is made in God's image. Every person is made for a relationship with God. Every person has value. But evidence that our society denies this truth is abundant. Planned Parenthood clinics and videos. Court rulings that try to redefine marriage. On-air shootings, drive-by shootings, revenge shootings. Parents abandoning children. Would-be parents refusing to have children, before or after they've been conceived. Luxurious lifestyles that add to the suffering of the poor. These are all part of our society.

It's ironic that the family, the basic unit of society, is being undermined by many of the actions of our society. At a societal level, it's suicidal. Many of us have had essential experiences as teachers and as learners in our families. That's the first way God intended us to learn: in a family, and with the support of a family. But our society is actively undermining what it means to *be* a family. We see this in the denial of basic dignity to children, born and unborn, and we see it in attacks on the true meaning of marriage.

Thank God, there are good things about our society – we have much to be proud of – but we clearly live in a time and place when some of our fellow citizens act as though certain people do not have basic human dignity. And we, as Christians, share the job of teaching them that everyone does. A society that denies the dignity of any human being – young or old, born or unborn, of any intelligence level, from any continent or country, of any color – that society needs to learn a basic lesson. It needs to be taught that every human is created in God's image, and does have dignity, no matter what he or she looks like, thinks like, or moves like. And every one of us can help teach that lesson.

A lot of teaching involves something other than standing in front of a classroom lecturing. A lot of you who have spent time in classrooms know that you can hear a long lecture, but not learn much from it. And yes, the same is true with sermons. We learn in many different ways, and a lot of what we learn, we learn by example. People are watching us, and we're teaching them by example, even if we never say a word.

So as I said earlier – you're here. But you could be somewhere else. For some of us, just being here is teaching someone we know what matters to us. As a parish, as Christians, we need to keep showing up. This means literally, at Mass, at Christian formation classes. And at picnics.[27] And it also means we need to keep showing up in the debate – the public debate in our society

---

[27] For several years we've had a picnic at our parish after Mass on Catechetical Sunday. While I was preaching this homily, we knew the tables outside were loaded with food, waiting for us.

about what a family is, and about which human lives matter. Because they all matter, but not everyone has learned that lesson yet.

This week, we have a unique opportunity to enter this debate. Pope Francis will be in our country in a few days. He's coming to canonize a new saint and to attend the World Meeting of Families. Media attention will be directed at the Church's teachings about marriage, family, and other matters that are rooted in a valid understanding of human dignity. We will have opportunities – when talking person-to-person, on Facebook, by email, or however we interact with other people around us – to remind them that all humans have dignity, and that healthy families are essential to a healthy society.

We all learn in different ways, and we all teach in different ways as well. But all of us teach. Some of us teach by just showing up. Some of us teach by writing or speaking, some of us teach in other small ways in our everyday lives. And yes, some of us teach by what we typically mean when we say teaching. But no matter how we teach, we all need to pray that we can help those around us know that every human has dignity – God-given dignity. If we do, we will be teaching them something that really matters. And by our example, and with his help, we can lead others closer to the master teacher, Jesus himself.

BEING A GOOD DOG
Luke 16:13

Twenty-fifth Sunday in Ordinary Time, 18 Sept 2016

Dogs do a lot of interesting things. They growl and bark. They wiggle and wag their tails. They defend their territory, after they've marked their territory. There are good dogs, and bad dogs. I want to tell you about a good dog.

This dog's name was Hachiko, and he lived in Japan in the early 20th century. His master was a professor who would ride the train to the university in the morning, teach his classes, and then ride back home in the evening. Hachiko would always be waiting at the train station to meet his master when he returned.

One evening, Hachiko went to the station, but his master didn't get off the train. The professor had died suddenly that day while he was at work. But the next day, Hachiko came anyway to meet the train at the normal time. And he came again the next day, and the next, and the next. And he continued to come every day for years to meet the train, even though his master never appeared again.

What does it mean to show true devotion to a master? This is the question a devoted servant would ask – how do I show that I love my master? Hachiko showed his devotion by consistency, by being there every day, waiting for his master. This is the role of a servant – being ready to greet and serve their master.

As Christians, we're servants. We might resist that label. We might forget, since we so often live life making our own decisions, but we're all called to be servants of God – to show him our devotion, and to wait on him. We're warned in today's gospel not to show devotion to the wrong master. Jesus said that we cannot serve God, our true master, if we're serving mammon. We will be devoted to one and despise the other, says Jesus.

But what is mammon? It's not an everyday word. Well, mammon can be defined as wealth, or material goods, or maybe simply things, or stuff. So ask yourself: are you a servant of God, or of things? What do you spend your time waiting for: Jesus, or wealth? Do you love God or money?

Being a servant of mammon doesn't necessarily mean we have a lot of mammon. It doesn't mean that we're rich or have a lot of stuff, though some of us do. It just means that we're devoted to it – it's what we spend our time waiting for, it's what we spend our lives trying to obtain, whether we're successful or not.

Mammon is sometimes capitalized, and the word has been used in some places as the name of a god – a personification of material wealth. So it makes sense for Jesus to say that we can't serve both – if Mammon is thought of as another god competing with the true God for people's attention and loyalty. Making God first in our lives is fundamental to our faith. The first of the 10 commandments says, "you shall have no other gods...." And Jesus said the greatest commandment was to love the Lord with all your heart and soul and mind.

Dogs... are good at showing when they love their master. They might not wait at a train station every day, but most of us know what a happy dog looks like. I know some people might not like being compared to a dog – if so, think about it this way: if all Christians are called to be servants, who are the ones who are most happy to serve their master? Which ones appear to be most in love with their master, and not at all attracted to the false god Mammon? We call those people saints, and if you learn stories about their lives, you'll know what it looks like when a person is really in love with God, and really understands what it means to serve him.

Something about saints, and about us, is that we're all different. Saints all love God, but they find different ways of showing it. Some enter a monastery and live hidden, quiet lives. Some chose a profession that allows them to serve others. Some marry and have children and spend their lives caring for their families. And there are many other pathways. We're all called to be servants of God, but how each one of us does that will look a little different.

No matter what path we take, though, being a servant of Mammon will prevent us from being a servant of God. I recently read a description of the problem that puts it this way: "...we are slaves of many superficial appetites that our modern consumer world teaches us to deem necessities, though they are not...."[28]

Those words came from a Carthusian monk preaching to his brother monks – a group of men who surely live a life more separated from the modern consumer world than us. And those words came from a sermon preached in

---

[28] From *The Spirit of Place: Carthusian Reflections*, 1998, Darton, Longman and Todd, p. 5.

1991, before the Internet and smartphones arrived to give us even more superficial appetites, and more ways to feed them.

We are servants – but unlike many slaves, we can choose who we serve. So who do we choose? Who's the master we're waiting on at the end of every day? The false god Mammon, or the true God, the living God, the God we meet here in this Eucharist?

Hachiko, the faithful dog, finally died after nine years of waiting for his master every day. He had become famous in Japan, and not long before he died a statue of Hachiko was erected at the train station where he waited. Films have been made about him in Japan, India, and the United States. Several books have been written about him... and he has been mentioned in at least one sermon at a small Catholic Church in Virginia. Pretty good for a dog.

What about us? What will we be known for once we're gone? Will it be for loving Jesus like the saints? Will people remember us for our devotion to Mammon? or God?

FROM MISERY TO FAITH
Habakkuk 1:3

Twenty-seventh Sunday in Ordinary Time, 2 Oct 2016

Sometimes children ask funny questions. And some of their funny questions are questions they ask God. For example:

- God if you made everything, why didn't you make my bed?
- God, are you really invisible, or is that just a trick?
- God, did you mean for the giraffe to look like that or was it an accident?
- God, in Bible times, did they really talk that fancy?
- God, I went to a wedding and they kissed right in Church. Is that OK?[29]

Adults ask God questions, too, but often our questions aren't quite as funny. Once we get older, and learn more about the way the world is, our questions can get pretty serious. In today's first reading we hear one of God's prophets, a man named Habakkuk, asking God a very serious question: "God, why must I look at misery?"

We don't know much about Habakkuk, though we do know he lived around the end of the 7th century BC in the kingdom of Judah. It was a difficult time. His nation had suffered from a split into north and south, and unlike our nation, it hadn't reunited after the split. Instead, the northern kingdom had been defeated by foreign invaders, and now Judah was being threatened by both internal corruption and foreign enemies.

But despite this uneasy situation, many of the people of Judah continued to abuse one another and ignore God. Habakkuk looked around him at his nation and said, "Destruction and violence are what I see... justice is numb, and perverted." And after seeing this violence, and the abuse of the weak and poor, he asked God this question: "why must I look at misery?"

If you've never felt like asking God that question yourself, you have been fortunate. You have perhaps also never watched the news, or read it on the Internet, or in a newspaper. Just think about this past week.

---

[29] I found these all on the Internet at multiple sources.

• Last Tuesday In El Cajon, California, police were called when a man was seen acting strangely behind a restaurant. When they arrived, he pointed a vaping device at them, and he was shot and killed, and nighttime protests followed. God, why must I look at misery?

• On Thursday, Indian jets attacked Pakistani positions along the shared border between those two nations; India called the attacks surgical strikes designed to stop terrorism. Pakistan reported two soldiers dead and many civilians deserting their homes, fleeing for their lives. God, why must I look at misery?

• In Hoboken, New Jersey, also on Thursday, a commuter train crashed inside a station where people were waiting during rush hour to go to work. One person was killed, and more than 100 were injured. God, why must I look at misery?

• In Syria, a ceasefire agreement was ignored as bombs were dropped on the city of Aleppo. Civilians were killed, including children. Russia said Friday that they were sending more warplanes; one US official said that the ceasefire was on life support, apparently not intending to be ironic. God, why must I look at misery?

• And in the Caribbean, Hurricane Matthew reached Category 5 this weekend, and is headed for Jamaica, Haiti, and Cuba tomorrow. So in case you've missed it, that's some of the news from the past week. God, why must I look at misery?

It's a question that makes sense to us – even without considering our individual struggles. And if you have some personal matter that's making your life difficult, so that you're too busy with your own problems to even listen to the news – then you might have your own private reasons to say, God, "why must I look at misery?"

The reason for this litany is not to depress us. It is to make clear that this question that Habakkuk asked God is just as relevant to us as it was to him. Habakkuk's question grew from his experience of the world, but it was also inspired by God, and preserved for over 25 centuries, and is now part of our scriptures. And for all those years God's people have continued to look around themselves, and then ask, "God, why must I look at misery?"

And guess what? God can take it. God can take our frustration, our anxiety, our anger, our grief. God already knows what we're thinking, and how we're feeling. And if we're frustrated about what's happening in the world around us, or in our own lives, if we're angry or afraid about something that millions of other people know about, or about something that no one else knows about – God knows, just as he has always known. And one thing the prophet Habakkuk learned, and the other prophets learned, and the apostles learned, and saints in every generation have learned, is that God doesn't always hide us from misery.

Many of us are blessed – with wonderful families, and friends, and material wealth. And we should never discount them or fail to give thanks for our blessings. For most of us, life is not all misery. But neither is it all pleasure. And God has never promised that it would be. So what did he say to Habakkuk when he asked this question – and what does he say to us when we ask, "God, why must I look at misery?"

The answer that we hear, the bottom line – and in the case of this reading, literally the last line – is this: "The just one, because of his faith, shall live."[30] Sometimes that has been reworded to read, "the just shall live by faith." And this answer, this concept, that God's people are called to live by faith, is central to the Christian life. We're not called to live a life of guarantees. We're not promised that God's going to fix the weather and get rid of the bad guys. We can ask why, but sometimes there's no simple answer.

Habakkuk is a small book, only three chapters. But that doesn't mean it's not important. And this answer from God – "the just shall live by faith" – is one of its key statements. It was quoted several times by New Testament writers, and it has become basic to a Christian understanding of life.

Near the beginning of the book of Romans Paul wrote, "I am not ashamed of the gospel. It is the power of God for the salvation of everyone who believes... in it is revealed the righteousness of God from faith to faith; as it is written, 'The one who is righteous will live by faith.'" And in the letter to the Galatians, Paul wrote, "no one is justified before God by the law... for the one who is righteous will live by faith." And the author of Hebrews wrote, "...my just one shall live by faith.... We are not among those who draw back and perish, but among those who have faith and will possess life."[30]

We're called to live by faith. And living the life of faith means praying and worshiping, and sharing the good news of Jesus with others, and seeking

---

[30] Romans 1:16-17, Galatians 3:11, and Hebrews 10:38-39.

peace and justice, and doing these things even when we're not getting answers to the difficult questions in our lives. We're not here because we have all the answers, but because the just shall live by faith.

God did promise Habakkuk that his people's enemies would be defeated, but he didn't say when. In a way that's our position, too. The solutions to some of the troubles we see in the world will come, but they might not come soon, and we might not see them. But the just shall live by faith, not by easy victories or guaranteed results.

This is not a defeated attitude. We do know certain truths, and we proclaim them. God's justice is inevitable. And when we deal with tragedy or evil, we aren't called to give up. We are called to try to make the world better. But sometimes, even after our best efforts, things aren't going the way they should. And even then, the just shall live by faith.

Asking God questions is not a problem. Sometimes we get clear answers, and sometimes we don't. Sometimes the answers take longer than we'd like, and sometimes we don't like the answers.

Children do ask funny questions. But in God's eyes, we're all children. His children. So keep asking God questions. He is our loving father, and even if we don't always understand the answers we get or get the answers we want... the just shall live by faith.

JONAH'S SECOND CHANCE
Jonah 3:1-10

Tuesday of the Twenty-seventh Week in Ordinary Time
6 Oct 2015

People love second chances. If we're playing a game and we mess up, we like to get a second chance. When kids get in trouble, they like it when their parents give them a second chance. This afternoon, I gave a biology exam – and I'd bet that some of my students would like a second chance to take that test right now. Today's first reading is a great second chance story.

Most of us know the story of Jonah being swallowed by a whale, or a big fish. That story was told in yesterday's first reading at Mass. And today we hear what happened next – which is that God gave Jonah a second chance. God told Jonah to go preach in Nineveh, but Jonah didn't want to. He tried to run from God – and he ended up in a fishes' belly. Running from God is never a good idea. But God gave Jonah a second chance. The fish spit him out, and so our reading today begins this way: "the word of the Lord came to Jonah the second time." And the second time, Jonah did what God wanted him to do.

This might seem like an unbelievable story – if we think too much about the big fish. But if we think about second chances, and think about the rest of the Bible, and think about our lives, we're reminded of something about God. God gives lots of second chances. Or as my students might say, God is all about second chances.

Well, he might not be all about them, but God's willingness to give us a second chance has been part of our relationship with God since the very beginning of time. Go all the way back to the beginning – the story of Adam and Eve. God gave them everything they needed, and very few rules, but they did what God told them not to do. God sent them out of Eden, but he didn't destroy them and replace them with new humans who would obey him. He gave Adam and Eve a second chance. That's a picture of all of us – every human who's ever lived.

What about the people of Israel? God saved them from slavery; he sent plagues, he led them through the Red Sea, he destroyed the Egyptian army, all for them – but before long, they were worshiping a statue of a cow. But God gave them a second chance, too.

Even the passion and death of Jesus was followed by the great second chance of the resurrection. People like Peter, who betrayed Jesus, or the ones who ran away when he was arrested, or even the ones who killed him – they were all given a second chance to follow him when he rose from the dead. And the same thing is true for us. God gives us all a second chance. And often a third chance, and a fourth chance, and more….

When have we heard the voice of the Holy Spirit, telling us something we should do – and then run the other way, like Jonah? When we're tempted to do that, we might want to remember that it's probably no fun trying to live in the belly of a fish. But the fish spit Jonah out. God gave him a second chance. And the same God who spoke to Jonah is the one who speaks to us, and he gives us second chances as well.

NOT CHANGING WHAT CAN'T BE CHANGED
Matthew 22:15-21

Twenty-ninth Sunday in Ordinary Time, 19 Oct 2014

Recently I haven't been able to avoid thinking about the ongoing debate concerning the meaning of marriage and the family. Students have asked me about it, and we've discussed it in classes. The secular media, as well as media outlets associated with the Church, have been talking about it. Our Church's cardinals and bishops have been discussing it as they've met in Rome in recent days.[31]

Those who suggest that marriage should be redefined remind me of the two groups who came to Jesus in today's gospel. They weren't seeking the truth; they were trying to win an argument. Should we pay taxes or not? As the gospel says, "they plotted how they might entrap Jesus in speech." We know what Jesus said: give to Caesar what is Caesar's, and to God what is God's. But what can we learn from the attitudes of those who were asking this question?

Today we're faced with a similar situation. Many people aren't seeking the absolute truth about marriage so much as they're trying to make the Church change to match their point of view. They have their minds made up. They come to Jesus, or to his Church, not to find truth, but to win an argument.

Governments in some parts of our nation, including, recently, our own state, have changed laws that address marriage. People are saying that marriage should be redefined by the Church to match their point of view, or to match the recent legal changes. But – give to Caesar what is Caesar's, and to God what is God's. In the context offered by today's gospel, it's worth remembering what marriage really is. Marriage is a sacrament. And sacraments are gifts. They are given to us by God; they aren't made up by people to suit our attitudes and desires. A sacrament is not something we as humans can redefine, so we can't redefine marriage.

We can, and we should, try to understand more about what marriage is. We should seek to learn more about it as a sacrament. It is what it is, a sacramental

---

[31] A reference to the first Synod on the Family that was held in Vatican City 5-19 October 2014.

union of a man and a woman. Like all sacraments it's a source of grace. And it's also a sign of God's love for us, the Church. It signifies the relationship, the covenant, between Christ and the Church. The Catechism refers to a marriage as indissoluble because it's made by God, and it represents things that will never be broken, including the promises of God to us, as well as the very nature of God.

A sacramental marriage between a man and a woman – the only kind there is – represents God, who is One, joined together with his Church – not two Gods joined together, or two Churches joined together. And a marriage between a man and a woman may produce children, and so also serve as an icon of the Holy Trinity – the Father and Son, from whom proceed the Holy Spirit, in an indissoluble union.

Now I'm not naive. I know that in our society we recognize what we call civil, or legal, marriages. People are routinely married sacramentally and legally at the same time. This has no doubt caused some of the confusion we're dealing with today. But no matter what a court or a legislative body says, the sacrament of marriage cannot be redefined to include anything other than one man and one woman, even if the legal definition changes 100 times. Give to Caesar what is Caesar's, and to God what is God's.

I also know, as you do, that two people who have been married – truly, sacramentally married – don't always represent the relationship between God and his Church in the way they should. Families don't always represent the Trinity in the way they should. And we know that people experience all sorts of desires that influence their attitudes towards marriage, and their behavior within marriage. But our human weaknesses don't change what marriage is, or what any of the sacraments are. That includes reconciliation, another source of grace and mercy, that can help us deal with our desires when they aren't what they should be.

As we think about marriage, and ask what it truly is, in the light of the gospel, we can ask a related question, one that might be more directly relevant for some of us today. What do we want when we come to an encounter with Jesus? Are we seeking the truth? Or do we think we already have it?

Here we are, at Mass. And we encounter Jesus here, in his Word, and in the Eucharist. But are we seeking an encounter with God? or are we trying to win an argument? Do we really think we're going to trap Jesus with our words? That we're going to rationalize our way around some truth that he's given us, or talk him out of something he's called us to do in our lives? Are we trying to change Jesus' mind? Or are we letting Jesus change us? Marriage, and the Eucharist, and all the sacraments, are meant to change us for the better. They're here to change us – we're not here to change them. We can't make them mean what we want them to mean. We can explore the depth of meaning they have for us.

The Bible begins with the story of Adam and Eve together in the Garden, where they were told to be fruitful and multiply. It's not exaggerating to say that all of human history and culture has been shaped by marriages. And the end of time itself is portrayed in the Bible as a wedding feast. Are we here today to get ready for that final marriage?

The Eucharist is intended to help us, the Church, prepare to become the bride of Christ at the end of time. The Eucharist, like marriage, and like all the sacraments, is what it is. May we receive them from God as he has given them, and give to Caesar what is Caesar's, and to God what is God's.

UNITY IN THE TRINITY
Ephesians 2:19-22

Tuesday of the Twenty-ninth Week in Ordinary Time
21 Oct 2014

"In the name of the Father and of the Son and of the Holy Spirit." When we begin Mass or any prayer like that – and by crossing ourselves – we affirm our belief in the Trinity: God as Father, Son, and Holy Spirit. And any time we recite the Creed, we say that we believe in the three persons of the Trinity. The Catechism says that our prayer is always a communion with the Holy Trinity,[32] and that we're part of a Church that originated in the plan of the Holy Trinity.[33] And while the word "Trinity" isn't used in the New Testament, the understanding of One God as three Persons is embedded in many New Testament passages, and we hear one of them in today's reading from Ephesians.

One of the themes of Paul's letter to the Ephesians is the unity of the Church. Ephesians was written to Gentile Christians, non-Jewish people who had come to believe that a Jewish rabbi was the basis for their salvation. The Gentile believers and the Jewish believers were joining together to form a single Church – one body, as Paul describes it, "built upon the foundation of the Apostles and prophets...." And one of the features of this Church was its developing understanding of the Trinity: not only the idea that God is three Persons, but also the idea that these three Persons are all integral to the nature of the Church.

Mentioning God in a Jewish context implies the unique creator God of the Old Testament who had given special status to the Jewish people. Paul, who was a Jew himself, says that both Jews and Gentiles have access in the Spirit to the Father, and that both had become "fellow citizens... and members of the household of God." Paul also describes the Church as having Christ Jesus as its capstone and adds that "through him the whole structure is held together and grows into a temple sacred in the Lord." And then Paul says, "you also are being built together into a dwelling place of God in the Spirit."

So in these few verses we hear God described as the Father, and the Son, and the Holy Spirit, all more than once, precisely where Paul is teaching that the Church is built of different people bound together into one structure. So whatever the Church is, it's connected to the idea of God as Trinity. The

---

[32] *CCC*, 2655.
[33] *CCC*, 758.

unity of the Church is related to the unity of the Trinity. One God; three Persons. One Church; a diversity of persons. This truth was essential to the Church from its earliest days, and it's essential for us today.

CONVENIENT OR INCONVENIENT
2 Timothy 4:2

Twenty-ninth Sunday in Ordinary Time, 16 Oct 2016
Our Lady of Mt. Carmel, Newport News, VA

Anybody stop at a convenience store this morning? 7-Eleven? Kangaroo? Wawa? They're pretty great, aren't they? You can get gas for your car, a sandwich for lunch, some coffee to drink now, something else to drink later on at home, magazines, medicine, and lots more, all in one spot. Very convenient... I guess that's why they're called convenience stores.

We like things that make our lives easy, and we surround ourselves with them. But despite all the ways we have to make life more convenient, sometimes it gets inconvenient. The convenience store... runs out of hot dogs. A student gets sick... the night before a test. Your child gets sick... just after the other one got well. Your car has a dead battery... the morning of a job interview. We all have examples.

And if you're living a committed Christian life, you've probably noticed that some inconvenient moments come along just because we're Christians. Especially when it comes to talking to other people about Jesus or putting our faith into action. But we just heard the words of Paul telling Timothy to proclaim the word... "whether it is convenient or inconvenient. And we're called to do the same."

A lot of times, living a genuine Christian life isn't convenient. And I'm not just talking about where we buy our gas and our hot dogs. In daily life, it's often more convenient to go along with the crowd than to do what our conscience and our Church tell us is the right thing to do. We're used to convenience in our everyday lives, but as Christians we're often called to do what's not convenient. And avoiding inconvenience has led to problems – for us as individual Christians, and for us as a nation.

Think about what's being said today in our country about health care, or marriage, or birth control, or how we treat the homeless or refugees, or how we care for our environment. How did we get to this point? I'm afraid that convenience has something to do with it.

- It's inconvenient to take care of the terminally ill. It would be more convenient to let them die... or help them die.

- It's inconvenient to get married or have a baby. It would be more convenient to use contraception, or to have an abortion.

- It's inconvenient to go somewhere and help someone build something and get sore and dirty; it's more convenient just to send money.

- It's inconvenient to stop and talk to that homeless guy for a few minutes or take him out to lunch. It's more convenient to pretend you don't see him.

- It's inconvenient to help that person who always seems to take twice as long as everyone else.

- It's inconvenient to pray with your family.

- It's inconvenient to teach your kids about God.

- It's inconvenient… to do a lot of things. But a lot of those inconvenient things are just what Christians should do.

Christianity is not a trip to the convenience store.

We aren't called to live the Christian life if it's convenient, or when it's convenient. Paul didn't tell Timothy to proclaim the gospel only when it was convenient – he said, whether it's convenient or inconvenient….

And proclaiming the truth about Jesus is something all Christians are called to do. One of the decrees of Vatican II says, "…all the faithful… proclaim the perfections of him who has called them out of darkness into his marvelous light."[34] All the faithful. Proclaiming the word whether it's convenient or inconvenient is part of normal Christian life, and there are as many ways to do it as there are Christians.

So if we're all called to proclaim the gospel, even when it's not convenient – how will you proclaim the gospel later this week? When you're at school, or at work… or at the convenience store… or just driving down the road in that wonderful I-64 traffic? Or when you're the only person in the group who

---

[34] The Decree *Presbyterorum Ordinis*, section 2. English translation available at www.vatican.va.

agrees with what the Church teaches? Or when your friend does something you both know is wrong?

It can help at times like that to remember the saints. It was not convenient for Damien of Molokai to be sent from Belgium to Hawaii to live and die with lepers. It wasn't convenient for Joan of Arc to leave her home and live with soldiers and be imprisoned and burned at the stake. It wasn't convenient for Thomas More to lose his position in the English government and be imprisoned in the Tower of London and then be beheaded. Chose any saint. Read their life story, and you'll find how inconvenient it can be to follow Jesus.

But most of all, it will help us if we think about Jesus. It was not convenient for Jesus to lay aside his divinity and become human. It was not convenient to stay up all night in the Garden of Gethsemane praying… and then to hear the soldiers coming. It was not convenient for Jesus when he felt nails being hammered through his hands. But his story doesn't end with the cross. Jesus is alive, and he knows that we struggle with the inconvenient moments in our lives. And he meets us in the scriptures, and in each other, and in the sacraments.

For grace and strength to proclaim the truth even when it's not convenient, we meet Jesus in the Eucharist. But when we do avoid the inconvenient path of truth, and take the convenient way of the world, even when we know better, we have something to confess. And when we seek reconciliation, we will experience mercy. Jesus is waiting to forgive us when we make our Christian lives merely lives of convenience.

Not long-ago Matthew Kelly wrote a book in which he told a story about a man who was inconvenienced.[35] This man was on a trip and on the day he was set to fly home, he was rushing with his friends to catch a cab to the airport. They had just enough time to get there without missing their flight, but as he ran down the sidewalk, he bumped into something, and when he looked back, he realized he'd knocked over a table of fruit that a lady was selling.

He was tempted to just keep running. He knew he'd miss his cab and probably his flight if he stopped, and it was going to be a huge inconvenience… but he did stop.

---

[35] I first encountered this story in the Prologue of Kelly's book *Rediscover Jesus: An Invitation*, 2015, Beacon Publishing, but since then I've seen various versions of it online. I'm not sure where it originated.

As he went back to pick up the fruit that he'd knocked over he noticed that the lady selling the fruit was blind. And she was crying. And the man said, "it's OK, it's OK," and he paid her for the damaged fruit, and then turned to walk away. But as he did, the lady said to him, "Mister, are you Jesus?" And he said, "Oh, no." And she said, "I only ask because I prayed for Jesus to help me as I heard my fruit falling all over the sidewalk."

The man did miss his plane, and he was stuck in that city until the next day. But all that night as he lay in his hotel room, he kept thinking – when was the last time someone had mistaken him for Jesus?

How about you? When was the last time you did something inconvenient that made someone mistake you for Jesus? If we rush through life, only doing what's convenient – we might never get mistaken for Jesus. But if we do stop, and share the gospel even when it's not convenient, maybe we will.

YOU'RE BEING WATCHED
Luke 14:1

Friday of the Thirtieth Week in Ordinary Time, 30 Oct 2015
Theological College, Washington DC

So, there's a new *Star Wars* movie coming out in December. When I read today's gospel, I was reminded of a moment in one of the earlier movies, *The Empire Strikes Back*. It's when Luke and R2-D2 have landed on a swampy planet and are about to set out in search of Yoda, the Jedi Master that Luke has been told about. Luke is setting up camp, then he pauses and says to R2-D2, "I feel like... like we're being watched." And he spins around, and there's Yoda, the one he was looking for, watching him – although Luke didn't recognize him at the time.

Have you ever had that feeling? Like you're being watched? Because you are.

Maybe it's obvious. We watch each other all the time, and we know other people watch us. If we walk around in clerical garb, we're going to be watched. If we tell people we're Christians, much less seminarians or deacons or priests, we're going to be watched. And if we act like we should be acting, like people who are trying to become saints, then we're going to be watched.

Have you ever tripped and fallen, then stood up quickly and looked around to see who was watching? If you're lucky, maybe no one saw you – but if you're unlucky, maybe a whole crowd was watching, and laughing, and you were embarrassed.

Jesus went to dinner, and the gospel makes a point of telling us that he was being watched carefully. Was he embarrassed? No. He healed a man, and then he told two parables. One of those parables we heard in today's gospel. It's a parable about humility – and it's also a parable about being watched, and potentially being embarrassed. Jesus was being watched, so he told the ones watching him a parable about how we should act when we're being watched.

Jesus knew he was being watched, and he used the attention he was getting to try to lead people closer to a true understanding of who he was: a healer, a teacher, and someone who challenged the accepted way of doing things when that interfered with people getting closer to God. Jesus didn't have to say that he felt like he was being watched. He knew he was. And Jesus was who the dinner guests were looking for, even if they didn't recognize him at first.

Jesus used people's attention to try to draw them closer to him. And so should we.

Jesus knew he was being watched. And so are we.

WHEN SOMETHING GETS LOST
Luke 19:1-10

Thirty-first Sunday in Ordinary Time, 30 Oct 2016

I was at a play performance recently when the lady sitting in front of me started acting very strangely. She was looking to her right and left, and bending over, shaking her head and muttering, and finally she stood up right in front of me when I was trying to watch the play. She kept looking around frantically, then left her seat and walked to the back of the room and started making calls on her cell phone. It was fairly distracting – even though the play was *The Hobbit*, and I had a pretty good idea how it would end.

Once Smaug the dragon had been killed, and the dwarves had their gold, and the lights were on again, this lady returned to her seat, still frantic. She was walking around talking to people, and finally she came over to me and told me what the problem was. She had lost a gold necklace. It was a necklace that her husband had brought to her when he returned home from a tour of duty in Iraq. It had great sentimental value for her. She had put it on earlier that evening to wear it to the play – and now it was lost.

Have you ever had that feeling? Have you lost something valuable to you and spent time searching frantically for it? It's not a pleasant feeling. At the end of the story of Zacchaeus, in today's gospel, we hear these words of Jesus: "the Son of Man has come to seek and to save what was lost." Only what was lost in this story was not a necklace. It was a soul. And, unlike an inanimate object such as a necklace, we can respond to the search of Jesus, and to his call. Like Zacchaeus, we can climb a tree – figuratively, at least. The question is what we do when Jesus calls us to come down.

Luke is the only gospel that tells the story of Zacchaeus, and one of the significant details he includes was that Zacchaeus was a short man. You know that when you lose something, it's often harder to find it if it's small than if it's large. I remember once dropping a small metal spring on the carpet in my father's study. Even though I knew exactly where I'd dropped it, it disappeared into the carpet and I never found it.

But in the case of Zacchaeus, he wasn't just physically short, and it wasn't just a physical search. Zacchaeus was also short on respect from those around him. They called him a sinner. According to the gospel he was a chief tax collector, and although we hear of other tax collectors in the scriptures, he is the only one who is called a chief tax collector. His cooperation with the

Romans who were oppressing his fellow Israelites made him short on friends. And Zacchaeus himself admits that his extortionist behavior has been short of ideal, ethically speaking. But despite all his literal and figurative shortness – which might seem to make him harder to find and save – Jesus does not hesitate to call out to Zacchaeus. And Zacchaeus responded immediately.

Perhaps at times we might identify with Zacchaeus. We might feel small and lost in the crowd. We might feel that we have fallen short of our own standards, or God's. Perhaps we simply feel lost – lost in sin, lost in life in general. When we do, it is helpful if we remember how good Jesus is at finding what he's looking for.

First, we can remember that Jesus knows who he's looking for. Jesus didn't walk into Jericho and say, "who's that guy up in the tree?" He called him by name: "Zacchaeus, come down quickly." And Jesus knew that Zacchaeus had ample room in his home: Jesus said that he had to stay with Zacchaeus that night, without asking if that was possible. Like Zacchaeus, Jesus knows each of us as well, and he knows our situations, no matter how far out on a limb we might feel ourselves to be. He knows you, and me, perfectly. He knows who he's looking for.

Also, remember that Jesus knows how to find us, and he meets us where we are. Even if we're up a tree, or perhaps especially if we are. Jesus was passing through Jericho on his way to Jerusalem. In the narrative of Luke's gospel, Jesus never passes through Jericho again. This was a unique opportunity for Zacchaeus, and Jesus made it possible. Jesus meets us where we are – in our shortness, our inadequacies, our worries, our frustrations, our sins.

We should also remember that Jesus knows what we feel like when we are lost. Jesus was human. Jesus himself, hanging on the cross, said this: "My God, my God, why have you forsaken me?" Hanging and dying, Jesus himself felt abandoned. Jesus had humbled himself, made himself small. He humbled himself by taking on human flesh, and he humbled himself further by being willing to die for us.

At every Mass we re-present this sacrifice of Jesus. We do not merely symbolize his sacrifice, but we also do not sacrifice him again. His unique sacrifice is made present for us, again and again, and Jesus again and again humbles himself by coming to us under the form of bread and wine – simple, humble, small things that become his very body and blood. In this sacrifice we are reminded over and over how he comes to seek and save what was lost. He has never given up the search.

The lady I mentioned who lost her necklace… she told everyone what she had lost, and several people helped her look for it. Eventually, someone found it and returned it to her. At the end of the story of Zacchaeus, Jesus has clearly found what he was looking for: he says that salvation has come to Zacchaeus's house – he has been found.

Today we're each at a different place in our individual response to the call of Jesus in our lives. Maybe some of us identify with Zacchaeus, worried that we're getting lost in the crowd. Or, that we're disliked, or not accepted by those around us. Or maybe we think that in the past we've not been as quick to respond to Jesus as Zacchaeus was. Thank God, Jesus is still searching for us, and calling to us, today – it's not too late. So today, let's pray that our response to Jesus' search, his call, and his humbling of himself for us will be as immediate and as saving as that of Zacchaeus.

SHE REACHES OUT HER HANDS TO THE POOR
Proverbs 31:19-20

Thirty-third Sunday in Ordinary Time, 16 Nov 2014

One of my favorite songs by one of my favorite bands is "Crumbs from Your Table," by U2.[36]

I was reading something last week, and I found a statement that reminded me of that song. Here's what I read: "...the mere fact that some people are born in places with fewer resources or less development does not justify the fact that they are living with less dignity." Now, that second quote is a little more wordy than U2's lyrics, but it expresses a similar thought, and it comes from a more authoritative source. If you didn't recognize it, in a couple of minutes I'll tell you who wrote it.

Meanwhile, consider our first reading today, from the last chapter of the book of Proverbs, which describes an ideal, virtuous wife. The book of Proverbs begins and ends with chapters that feature parents speaking to their sons and encouraging them to seek wisdom, and to make wise choices, including wise choices about marriage. In the final chapter, the young man who presents the description of a virtuous wife is in fact a king, remembering the advice of his mother.

It's clear from the reading we heard that the wife described in Proverbs 31 is competent. It becomes even more clear if we read the entire chapter: She's economically astute; she's what we might call in contemporary language proactive in her business dealings. But she's not just smart and capable, she's also good – she's virtuous.

I want to focus on the part of her description that we hear in verses 19-20: "She puts her hands to the distaff, and her fingers ply the spindle. She reaches out her hands to the poor and extends her arms to the needy." Putting her hands to the distaff and plying the spindle means that she's spinning, making thread or yard to be used for clothing. So she's described first as working to provide for her own family – but then as going out to the poor to whom she

---

[36] And in the next sentence of the original homily I quoted lyrics from the song, which I can't do here for legal reasons. The song is on the album *How to Dismantle an Atomic Bomb*, released in 2004.

reaches out her hands as well. She uses her hands to work for her family's security, and then also to reach out to the poor.

We sometimes say charity begins at home, though that's not a Biblical phrase, and we need to be sure what we mean if we say that. Though charity might begin at home, it definitely shouldn't end there. Certainly it doesn't for the virtuous wife of Proverbs 31. Most of us, though, aren't kings in search of a virtuous woman to marry. But who are we? We're the Church, and we should remember that the Church is the bride of Christ, who is in fact a king, the king of the Universe. We are called to be a bride, and to be wise and virtuous, like the wife of Proverbs 31, as we await our wedding feast in heaven.

Now back to the quote from earlier: "the mere fact that some people are born in places with fewer resources or less development does not justify the fact that they are living with less dignity." In case you didn't recognize those words, I'll tell you now: they come from our Holy Father, Pope Francis. They're from his apostolic exhortation – a short book, really – called *The Joy of the Gospel* (*Evangelii Gaudium* in Latin).[37] It was published a little less than one year ago, on 24 Nov 2013, the end of the Year of Faith.

Why were such words appropriate at the end of the Year of Faith, and why are they still appropriate for us now, and why will they go on being appropriate for us? Because, as James says in his epistle, faith without works is dead. Because, as the virtuous wife of Proverbs shows us, our energy and resources aren't meant to be used entirely to guarantee our own security and comfort but should be shared with those in need. Because, as Pope Francis teaches us, our witness will be ineffective if we ignore those who need help.

Here are the words of Pope Francis again: "No one must say that they cannot be close to the poor because their own lifestyle demands more attention to other areas."[38] That speaks to us at the individual level, and the same truth applies at the congregational level, the parish level, as well. Pope Francis also said, "Any Church community, if it thinks it can comfortably go its own way without creative concern and effective cooperation in helping the poor to live with dignity and reaching out to everyone, will also risk be breaking down..."[39]

---

[37] See section 190.
[38] *Evangelii Gaudium*, section 201.
[39] *Evangelii Gaudium*, section 207.

Certainly the gospel reading we hear today also reinforces this point. The servant who buries his master's money, rather than investing it, is reprimanded. His entire focus was inward; he did not engage his community.

What about us? Our resources – our time, money, and abilities of many kinds – are all ultimately God's. We're the servants, not the master. It's hard just to acknowledge that sometimes. But we are. And how are we using what the Master has given us? If we're not reaching out our hands to the poor, and extending our arms to the needy, like the virtuous wife of Proverbs, we risk breaking down – as individuals, and as a community.

Today, I'm not promoting a single specific cause or organization. Many people in our world are in real physical need, and there are many ways to help them, individually, as a parish, and as part of the universal Church. I just want to encourage us all to be more sensitive to the call of scripture, and the call of our Holy Father, and the call of our Heavenly Father: not to ignore the poor, and to pray that we won't forget to reach out our arms to those who live in places with fewer resources, so that where they live will not decide whether they live or whether they die.

ZACCHAEUS THE FRUIT
Luke 19:1-10

Tuesday of the Thirty-third Week in Ordinary Time, 18 Nov 2014

Near the end of his first encyclical, *Lumen Fidei*, Pope Francis writes that "when our own spiritual lives bear fruit, we become filled with joy...."[40] In that encyclical he also describes faith repeatedly as a journey. We get a glimpse of a fruitful moment in one man's journey of faith, and the joy that comes from it, in today's gospel.

This short part of the journey of Zacchaeus that we hear about has lots of movement. Jesus is traveling through Jericho. Zacchaeus runs to a place where he can meet Jesus. Zacchaeus climbs up a tree to see Jesus. Zacchaeus climbs back down the tree when Jesus calls him. All this movement factually describes what happened when Zacchaeus met Jesus; but it also invites us to think about our own life journeys, and whether all our busy moving around puts us in position to meet Jesus.

The sycamore tree Zacchaeus climbed was a type of fruit tree – not the same as our sycamore trees.[41] In a way, Zacchaeus becomes the fruit of that fruit tree himself, and Jesus picks the fruit, which is obviously ripe for the picking. When Zacchaeus comes down, Jesus receives him, and Zacchaeus receives Jesus – with joy.

Zacchaeus immediately shows that his new relationship with Jesus will be fruitful; he promises to make amends for wrongs that he has done. He has already experienced joy in his encounter with Jesus, and he looks forward to more as their relationship continues.

If we seek joy in our lives, the words of Pope Francis and the story of Zacchaeus both suggest this: get closer to Jesus and be fruitful. Respond to the call of Jesus, do what he asks, and fruitfulness and joy will follow. As Catholics, one of the most important ways we meet Jesus, and prepare for what he has for us to do, is in the Eucharist – so we can rejoice – we're in the right place, and we're about to see Jesus!

---

[40] *Lumen Fidei*, section 58.
[41] By "our sycamore trees" I mean the American sycamore, *Platanus occidentalis*, which is a common tree where I live in central Virginia. The tree Zacchaeus climbed is thought to have been the widely cultivated sycamore fig, *Ficus sycomorus*.

GRUMBLE, GRUMBLE
Luke 19:7

Tuesday of the Thirty-third Week in Ordinary Time/
Memorial of St. Elizabeth of Hungary, 17 Nov 2015

Grumble, grumble, grumble. Grumble... is an interesting word. It almost sounds like what it means – it's onomatopoetic, as they say in English class. In the original Greek language of the New Testament, it's *goggyzo*. Sometimes it's translated murmur, or mutter. And in two places, both in the gospel of Luke, a special intensive form is used: *diagoggyzo*. One of those places is here in the story of Zacchaeus.

Jesus was showing mercy to a man who was despised by his society. Zacchaeus was called a chief tax collector, which meant that he worked for the oppressors of his people. He was a sell-out, a traitor, in many people's opinion. They called him a sinner. But Jesus called him down from his tree and went home to eat with him. And when they saw this, "they began to grumble."

Maybe this is a warning to us: if we act like we should, if we act like Jesus, there's a good chance we're going to make people grumble. Saints have had this problem. Today we honor St Elizabeth of Hungary; one biography says that "(h)er extraordinary generosity was sometimes criticized by others as extravagance,"[42] which sounds something like grumbling to me.

Maybe this story's also a warning for us when we feel the urge to grumble. In Exodus, not long after the people of Israel had escaped Egypt, they began to grumble because they didn't have water. Soon after that, they were grumbling because they didn't have food. In both cases God gave them what they needed; in fact, this is when he first provided them manna, the bread from heaven.

And when Jesus came, attempting to show his people a new way to live, they grumbled again – and his response involved food again. He ate with Zacchaeus, and people grumbled. Then, it wasn't too long before the Last Supper, when he gave his followers the bread from heaven, his own body.

---

[42] *Butler's Lives of the Saints, New Full Edition*, November volume, 2000, Burns & Oates/The Liturgical Press, p. 147.

The story of Zacchaeus is only found in Luke's gospel, and it's unusual in several ways. One is that intensive form of the word grumble. And both times this word is used, people were grumbling about the same thing – Jesus spending time with sinners. But that's who Jesus came to help, and the people didn't understand. The Israelites grumbled because they didn't trust God and understand his plan for them. People grumbled when Jesus ate with Zacchaeus because they didn't trust and understand him. If we're grumbling about what God is doing, maybe we should remember their example.

But if we're following the example Jesus gave us, we might need to be ready to hear some grumbling ourselves. And if people grumble, and murmur, and mutter about us long enough, it might mean we're headed the same place Jesus was to the Last Supper, and then to the cross.

LOOK AT THE CRUCIFIX
Luke 23:35-43

Solemnity of Our Lord Jesus Christ, King of The Universe,
21 Nov 2016

Look at the crucifix hanging here above us. Look at the crucifix, and ask yourself: "is this my king?"[43]

Look at the crucifix and think about two things:

- First, during the entire scene described in our gospel reading today, Jesus was hanging on the cross. Many people insulted him, one criminal reviled him, and another criminal had a conversation with him – all while Jesus was hanging and dying on the cross.

- And second, consider that this gospel reading that describes Jesus being executed along with two criminals is the very gospel that the Church gives us to proclaim on the feast of Christ the King.

Why do we look at the crucifix so intently on the same day we celebrate Jesus as king? How do we respond to this kind of a king, a king who was crucified?

Each one of us would answer these questions in different ways. But if we collect all our different answers together, there are really only two responses. When we think of the crucified Jesus as a king: we can either accept him or reject him. And we see those two responses represented in the gospel by the two criminals who were crucified with him.

We might say that one criminal believed in Jesus as his savior, and one did not, and that would be accurate. But we can be more precise than that. The one who did believe, believed specifically that Jesus was a king. Because what he said to Jesus was not just I believe in you, or please save me. What he said

---

[43] Protestant readers might not be aware that in nearly every Catholic church, including in my home parish where this was preached, a crucifix hangs over the altar. A crucifix has some sort of representation of the body of Christ on the cross, often a three-dimensional one, rather than being a bare cross as found in many Protestant churches.

was: remember me when you come into your kingdom. And who has a kingdom, but a king?

Look at the crucifix and consider that despite Jesus being shamed, and tortured, and executed, despite his body being dirty and torn, despite many of his friends abandoning him and many people mocking him – one criminal believed that he was a king. And he was. And he is.

The sign posted over his head as he was dying read King of the Jews. But calling Jesus the King of the Jews is really just a glimpse at who he was and is. Kings often have many titles, and Jesus does, too.

Today's feast is not called the Solemnity of Jesus Christ King of the Jews. It's not called the Solemnity of Jesus Christ King of the Church. And it's not even called the Solemnity of Jesus Christ King of the Earth. Today is the Solemnity of Jesus Christ, King of the Universe.

Jesus is King of the Universe because he made the universe. Look at the crucifix and remember: this man on the cross was also God, who created everything; "all things were created through him and for him. He is before all things...." That's what St Paul wrote to the Colossians. It sounds incredible, and outrageous. But who wants a predictable, ordinary King, or a predictable, ordinary God?

Jesus is also our king because by his death, he defeated death and the powers of death that threaten us and his kingdom. Three days after the crucifixion came the resurrection. He is not dead; he is risen. And we do not need to fear death because we can be like the criminal who believed in him: we can also look forward with hope to life with him forever.

Do we agree with the criminal who believed this, or the one who didn't? Those two criminals hanging there with Jesus had only a short time left to live; they had to show their faith, or their lack of it, through what they said. Their wills and their words were all they had left.

But we're not so limited. We act with great freedom in our lives. And as we go through each day, making choices, do we act as though we believe Jesus is our king, and the king of the Universe, or not?

Many people today would say that they believe that Jesus lived, and that he was crucified, but would also sneer at his claims to divinity – just as some did when he hung dying. Plenty of people believe Jesus lived and died without believing he was God, and without acknowledging him as their king. But if we Christians don't acknowledge Jesus as our king in the way we live our lives, then our lives will have the same practical effect as theirs.

What should we do, then, besides just saying that we believe Jesus is king? Talk is cheap, as the saying goes. Since we're not being crucified for our beliefs – not yet, anyway – since we can move and act freely, how should believe Jesus is king of the universe make any practical difference in our lives? Maybe we're not used to thinking about having a king. So if we want to live as good subjects of the king, it's good to look at the crucifix and remind ourselves what kind of kingdom Jesus established. Was it a kingdom like the ones we read about in fantasy novels, with castles and knights and dragons? No. Was it the kind the Jewish people looked for, as they sought relief from Roman rule, or the kind of political victory some people look for today? No.

The kingdom Jesus established and still rules is seen in the Church. The Church is a visible manifestation of his kingdom. The Catechism makes an even stronger claim: "Christ's kingdom... manifests its presence through the miraculous signs that attend its proclamation by the Church...."[44]

Miraculous signs? Yes. Certainly in the lives of the saints, and sometimes in the lives of the rest of us. Just because we might not see a miracle on any given day doesn't mean we're not part of a kingdom where they've been happening for 2000 years. Our king sent the Holy Spirit to the Church at Pentecost, and the miracles started, and He still comes, and they still happen.

And in giving us the Church, Jesus also gave us the sacraments that give us grace to live as members of this kingdom. The Eucharist brings us into contact with the sacrifice by which our king defeated death. Look at the crucifix and remember at Mass, his sacrifice is made present,[45] and the words of the criminals crucified with him are not just ancient history.

We're given the sacraments, and sometimes miracles, because the kingdom of Jesus is a kingdom at war. Jesus did not establish a typical kingdom with a typical army, but a Church, and for centuries we've been known as the Church Militant – the Church at war with evil.

This war is unusual for at least two reasons. The first is that this war is spiritual, not physical. That's why our weapons include prayer, the sacraments, the Bible, and the gifts of the Spirit, and not bombs and guns.

---

[44] *CCC*, 670.
[45] See *Ecclesia de Eucharistia* sections 12-13.

This war is also unusual because it has already been won, even though we're still fighting it. Look at the crucifix and remember: the crucified Christ soon became the risen Christ. Our king is not dead; he is alive. The cross that was meant to be a tool of death was used to defeat death itself.

This is why the cross is our sign, and the sign of his kingdom. This is one reason we hang crucifixes in our Churches – not just because they remind us of death, but because they remind us of the defeat of death. And we don't just hang crucifixes in our Churches. We carry them in our pockets and purses and backpacks, and when we bless ourselves, or any object, we use the sign of the cross. And when we look at the crucifix or make the sign of the cross, we remind ourselves, and our Enemy, that our king has won the war over death.

So are we good soldiers? Are we living as though we're members of a kingdom whose king has already won an eternal victory over death? Do we always value life over death? If we side with death over life, as so many in our culture do, we're mocking Jesus, like the criminal who hung there dying with him. If we don't promote life over death, and live in communion with the living Church, we're denying our king. We're giving strength to the enemy, and from an eternal perspective, we're on the losing side of the war.

So look at the crucifix again... look at the crucifix and ask yourself: "is he my King?"

LENT

PROPER HYDRATION
Isaiah 55:10-11

Tuesday of the First Week of Lent, 16 Feb 2016

Sunday night it snowed, and this morning it rained... it seems like a good day to think about these words from Isaiah:

> Just as from the heavens
> the rain and snow come down
> And do not return there
> till they have watered the earth...
> So shall my word be
> that goes forth from my mouth....

We know a few things about rain and snow. If we don't get enough, plants don't grow. Crops fail and people can go hungry. On the other hand, if we get too much and it doesn't soak into the soil, it doesn't do any good. Neither drought nor flood are good things. So the ideal is for the rain to soak into the ground and stay there until it's needed, and to be used gradually by the plants. The same seems to be true for God's word.

If we never heard God's word, if we never went to Mass or read the scriptures or studied the Bible, most of us realize that would be a problem. On the other hand, suppose you went to a conference or a week-long revival meeting and heard intense preaching and teaching for several days, so much that you were overwhelmed, but weren't able to absorb most of it. That wouldn't be ideal, either. God says his word should be like the rain in our lives. The right amount, not too much, not too little. Refreshing and leading to growth.

It's interesting that these words echo the words of Jesus from Sunday's gospel. When Satan tempted him to turn stones into bread, he said "we do not live by bread alone, but by every word that goes forth from the mouth of God." So the word of God is like our food and drink, and again we can realize that too little or too much are both problems. And so is the wrong kind of food or drink: eat or drink poison, and it will make us sick or kill us, not make us healthy.

We can see a model in all this: God's word is meant to be regularly consumed, in reasonable amounts. And the Church offers a way to do this: Mass, with readings, and the Liturgy of the Hours are two ways. This is a reason that the ministry of lector is important: you're helping serve others their food and drink, in just the context that it's meant to be received.

So as we watch the snow finish melting and the rain soak into the ground, it's good to remember that we should always be soaking ourselves in God's word. Not waiting until our lives are deserts and then performing some sort of emergency irrigation but keeping ourselves properly hydrated with the Word of God that will keep us from ever growing thirsty.

NOSTALGIA FOR A PLACE WE'VE NEVER BEEN
Psalm 137:1,4

Fourth Sunday of Lent, 15 Mar 2015

Think of a place from your past, a place you loved, but a place to which you can never return. Perhaps it was your home, or the home of someone you loved who is now gone. Maybe it was somewhere you worked or went to school years ago. Maybe it was a place you met someone special. Maybe it was a summer camp, a vacation spot, or a secret hiding place.

The feelings we have when we think of such places, we call nostalgia. The word nostalgia was invented in 1688, but this real, human feeling is much older than that. The word originally meant the same thing as homesickness, though today it seems to be used more loosely. Sometimes it simply seems to mean a fondness for old things, or even replicas of old things, and it's used to sell decorations to people waiting in line at restaurants, and souvenirs to people on vacation. But true nostalgia, a longing for a place where we once felt at home, is more than that, and this emotion flows from the Psalm we hear today.

"By the streams of Babylon we sat and wept when we remembered Zion. How could we sing a song of the LORD in a foreign land?" This is the voice of a Jewish poet remembering his home – the home he was taken away from when Babylon conquered his nation. The Hebrew people didn't have our word nostalgia, but they surely felt nostalgia, a homesickness for Jerusalem, for Zion, the homeland that God had given them.

It's appropriate that a psalm gives us such a clear expression of nostalgia. A song can often cause us to feel nostalgia. In fact, when I was beginning my preparations for this homily, I was in a shop drinking coffee, and all the music that was playing was from the 1980s. Then a song came on that was about remembering the 1960s...[46] And then I realized – I was experiencing nostalgia while listening to a song about nostalgia while preparing a homily about nostalgia.

---

[46] Which I quoted in the homily, but not here for legal reasons. The song was "Summer of '69," by Bryan Adams.

Now, I don't want you to think this homily was inspired by bad 80s music! or even good 80s music. But when music or a picture or anything else gives us such strong feelings, it seems reasonable to ask: "What good are they? Why has God made us so that we feel nostalgia?"

Sometimes we have nostalgia for a place we can never return to. And sometimes when we do return to a place we once knew, it has changed, and we feel uncomfortable. We feel that we've lost something. The Jewish people had this experience. After several decades, they did return to their homeland, but it was changed. The Christian Church, and in a way all of humanity, is like Israel. We feel nostalgia – we want to go home. And in a way, like Israel, we will. But can home ever be what it once was? And aren't we all from different places, anyway? Yes, and no.

All people were made to live in God's presence without sin – but we do not. We learn this truth from Genesis. In a way, we all have nostalgia for a time when we lived without sin. In a way, we all have nostalgia for Eden. But we can't go back there. First, it's not a literal place, and second, if it were, an angel with a flaming sword would keep us out!

But our nostalgia for the real places we have known is valid, and important, partly because it can point to something, we all share. It gives us a deep emotional sense that there is some place better than the here and now. And no matter what happens to the different earthly places we have loved; we all have a real hope of going home to an even better place. Just like the psalmist, we may shed tears when we remember places from our past. And just as a time came for some of the Jewish people to go home, such a time will come for us. But not to the homes of our past – which were not perfect, no matter how fondly we remember them. To put it simply, we're homesick for heaven.

This is one of the great promises of our faith – that we hope to live forever in heaven. If nostalgia is homesickness, but heaven is our real home, then our nostalgia for something in our past can be understood as a longing for something similar in our future. As Christians, we can understand this as a promise. We can even have hope that those people we knew in those places we remember will be there as well.

So is nostalgia good for us? It can be. It can be a reminder while we're here that we should live a certain way. It can be a reminder that our celebration of the Eucharist is a unique way of approaching heaven while we're still on earth. It can be a reminder that what we do on earth may make our path to heaven less uncertain. During Lent, we're asked to deny ourselves in our fasting and almsgiving. Maybe Lent is a good time to remember that during this life, we're also being denied our ultimate home, but that we have a real hope to go there one day. Our feelings of nostalgia for times and places on earth can be more than just memories of what we've lost; they can be redeemed and serve us as promises of an eternity in heaven.

JESUS IS GOD
John 10:31-42

Friday of the Fifth Week of Lent, 27 Mar 2015
Wren Chapel, College of William and Mary, Williamsburg, Virginia

Jesus of Nazareth, whose mother was Mary, whose adoptive father was Joseph, who lived 2000 years ago in what is now northern Israel, who spent the last few years of his life as a traveling teacher, and who was executed by the Romans who ruled his homeland – was God. And he is God.

This is one of the central claims of our faith: Jesus is God. If we don't believe this, no matter what else we do believe, we don't believe what Christians have believed since they first started to follow Jesus. I have no doubt that many of you – I hope all of you – would agree with this.

But despite the fundamental nature of this truth, that Jesus is God, we sometimes hear the question asked – "did Jesus ever claim to be God? Or is this something early Christians made up?" Today's gospel reminds us that Jesus did identify himself with God, but that he did not simply say "I am God," with no elaboration. Jesus did not speak abstractly when he affirmed his divinity. He used language and images that were relevant to his culture, and meaningful to the particular people he was talking to.

Clearly the religious leaders in today's gospel who wanted to kill Jesus had heard something that they understood as a claim of divinity. And Jesus did not respond to them by saying "wait, you misunderstood me!" Instead he referred to Psalm 82, part of the Hebrew scriptures that his accusers would recognize. He used a style of argument that they were familiar with. The answer Jesus gave when they accused him of blasphemy for claiming to be God was designed to defend this claim, not deny it. And it was given in a form that Jewish religious leaders could understand and relate to and remember – even if they did not agree with it.

Jesus says several things, in this gospel and elsewhere, that serve as claims of divinity. He also says that his identity should be judged based both on what he said and on the works he did, actions that his accusers could see for themselves, that would show that he was who he claimed to be. These were not theoretical arguments; they were meaningful actions in the lives of the people he lived with.

Jesus claimed to be God, and he was. His actions matched his words. We claim to be Christians. And our actions should match who we claim to be. Jesus pointed to his life as evidence that he was divine. Can we point to our lives as evidence that we are Christians? Do we identify ourselves as Christians not just with words, but in ways that are relevant and meaningful to the people we talk to every day?

PALMS IN OUR PALMS
John 12:12-13

Palm Sunday of the Lord's Passion, 20 Mar 2016

We have palms in our palms, and while holding our palms, we've just heard one of the longest, if not the longest, gospel reading of the entire Church year. The palms tell us it is Palm Sunday; the gospel describes the Passion and Death of Jesus, and so we also call today Passion Sunday.

During this long reading, if you were listening closely, you might have noticed that there was nothing specifically about palms; they're not mentioned in Luke's version of the triumphal entry of Jesus into Jerusalem that we just heard. But all four gospels tell us about this event, and it's John, and only John, who tells us that "when the great crowd that had come to the feast heard that Jesus was coming to Jerusalem, they took palm branches and went out to meet him...."

Why palms? What do palm branches mean? When I was a kid, we went for vacation several times to Myrtle Beach, South Carolina. One of the things that stood out to me, besides the fact that we were at the ocean, was the palm trees that grew there.[47] We didn't have palm trees back here in central Virginia.

Palms are mostly tropical, so palms have always represented warm places to me, and a lot of people. They also represent food and water, since palms often grow around an oasis in a desert, and since coconuts and dates come from palm trees. So in a broader sense palms represent health and life.

In the Roman Empire, when Jesus lived, champions of sporting events were given palms, so they also symbolized victory. And not just sports – military victories were also celebrated with palms. A victorious army would return home waving palm branches. In Christian art, palms have been used for many centuries to represent martyrs. The idea is that a martyr, by dying for their faith, has reached heaven – which is the ultimate victory in life.

Maybe when we get to heaven there will be palm trees growing; Revelation 7:9 refers to an uncountable multitude of people in heaven wearing white robes and holding palm branches in their hands. But what about Palm

---

[47] Also known as sabal palmettos or dwarf palmettos, *Sabal minor*, the state tree of South Carolina.

Sunday? What do the palms tell us today? What does this have to do with our celebration, and our movement through Holy Week this week?

We just heard in the gospel that many of those who were with Jesus at the beginning of the week, waving their palm branches, had abandoned him by the end of the week. So here we are, with him, at the beginning of the week, waving our palms. But will we be with him at the end of the week?

I think most of us – hopefully all of us – would say yes. When we think that next Sunday is Easter, we say "yes, I'll be here next Sunday." But remember Peter; he insisted that he would stay with Jesus and die with him – just before denying that he even knew him.

I doubt any of us will have the opportunity to gain the palm of martyrdom this week, though if we lived in some other parts of the world right now, I wouldn't say that. But I expect many of us will have the opportunity to put ourselves in Peter's shoes this week. We'll suddenly be asked a question, or put in an awkward position, and have to decide whether we're going to deny Jesus in our conversations, our daily activities.

Celebrating is fun and being warm and cozy is great. If that's what palms mean, we can enjoy them. But what if they mean self-denial, dying to ourselves, even dying for our faith? Waving our palms is easy on Palm Sunday. But what about the rest of the week, and what about the rest of our lives?

EASTER

KEEPING A SECRET, OR NOT
John 20:17; Acts 2:36, 39

Tuesday in the Octave of Easter, 7 Apr 2015

Secrets. There are different kinds of secrets. Sometimes people know secrets that should be kept, and never told, but they tell them anyway. And sometimes we know things that should be told, but we keep them a secret. Keeping secrets that need to be told can be unhealthy – bad for our bodies and our minds. Keeping secrets that need to be told can also be spiritually unhealthy.

The great truth that we're celebrating now – the Easter truth, the truth that Jesus was raised from the dead, is alive, and waiting to meet us all – is not meant to be kept secret. This is one message of both our first reading and our gospel tonight.

When Mary Magdalene met Jesus in the garden after his resurrection and didn't recognize him, he immediately spoke to her in a way that revealed his identity. And then he said to her, "Stop holding on to me, for I have not yet ascended to the Father. But go to my brothers and tell them...." Sometimes, depending on the translation we read or the images we see of this moment, we can be puzzled by his response and wonder if he was speaking harshly to Mary. But if we do, we might miss this emphasis: Jesus has shared the truth of his resurrection with Mary, and he wants her to immediately go and share it with others.

Likewise, shortly after the resurrection, Peter spoke to his Jewish brothers and sisters and said, "Let the whole house of Israel know for certain" who Jesus was. And not only the Jewish people; he adds a moment later that this promise is also made to "all those far off, whomever the Lord our God will call." Well, that includes us.

The message of Easter is not a secret. It spread like wildfire through the land of Palestine; we just read of Peter baptizing about 3000 people in one day. This is the opposite of a secret. The problem is when we act as though the truth of Jesus is a secret. We can hide this truth by not stating clearly what we believe. We can also hide it by acting in a way that is contrary to the model Jesus gave us.

Jesus is risen. As we continue our Easter celebration, as we receive the body of this same Jesus in the Eucharist, and go our into our daily lives in the days ahead, we can take confidence that this is no secret; this is Good News that we are meant to share with everyone.

A GHOST DOES NOT HAVE FLESH AND BLOOD
Luke 24:39

Third Sunday of Easter, 19 Apr 2015

Do you like ghost stories? When I was a little boy, I used to watch a cartoon on TV called *Casper the Friendly Ghost*. I don't remember it well; I actually remember my parents telling me that I watched it more than I remember the show. But of course now we have the Internet, and it turns out that episodes of *Casper the Friendly Ghost* are online. So last week, I did a little research.

Apparently, I didn't have very refined tastes in television when I was four years old. But I forgive myself.

In the show, Casper was not a normal ghost. The normal ghosts were all bigger and meaner than Casper. They only wanted to relate to humans by spooking them. But Casper wanted to be friendly. The problem is, whenever people or animals saw Casper, they saw a ghost. And ghosts are scary, so Casper had a hard time making friends.

Many ghost stories tell about someone who thinks they see a ghost. But what often happens is that they see something and aren't really sure what it is, and when they find out – it was a cat, or a shadow, or a tree branch scraping the window – not a ghost. Today's gospel is something like that. Jesus startled and terrified his disciples when he appeared to them, and they thought they were seeing a ghost. But they weren't. Yes, Jesus had died, but he had also risen from the dead. And he was no ghost. How did they know? Because a ghost does not have flesh and blood.

Jesus had a real physical body that his followers could touch. Many people have tried to explain away the Resurrection, and one way to do that is to say that Jesus did not have a real human body – that he was just a ghost. Early Christians had to fight against this belief, that Jesus was not truly human, but only appeared to be so – that he did not really have a body.

Maybe today it's more common to meet someone with the opposite confusion, who argues that Jesus was only flesh and blood, only human, and not God. The truth is, he is both – fully human and fully divine. But from the gospels we know Jesus did not have the same type of body after his Resurrection. He was changed – he could appear and disappear suddenly; he could talk to people who knew him but not be recognized. Yet he was still

Jesus, and he had a real body. We know he was not a ghost, and that the Easter story is no ghost story. Because a ghost does not have flesh and blood.

It's interesting that our English translation uses the word "ghost" here. In nearly all the oldest manuscripts of the gospel, the word used here is the same word that's used for "spirit" in many places in the New Testament. Maybe ghost seems to fit the idea that the disciples were frightened better.

But Jesus wasn't raised from the dead to spook anyone or haunt anyone. His life and resurrection are meant to give us an idea of how to live now, and what we can look forward to. The Resurrection of Jesus says something about Jesus – and, it also says something about us. It can give us comfort in our present lives and give us hope for our future. A ghost story can't do that. Because a ghost does not have flesh and blood.

We can take comfort that Jesus understands our lives, the limitations we face, in our flesh-and-blood bodies, because he lived in a body like ours. He understands fatigue and pain, stress and misunderstanding. But he also showed us how to enjoy these bodies; how to use them to love one another, to glorify God the Father, to reflect our creator God through creative, productive lives, to enjoy life on earth while we're living here.

Yes, human bodies have limits – but human bodies are good. Jesus became human, and this is one of the great messages of the Incarnation – that having a human body is good. God made us human and wants us to be human – with flesh and blood bodies – now, and after our resurrection. You were not made to be a ghost, because a ghost does not have flesh and blood.

The resurrection of Jesus is a promise of what ours will be like. The Apostle Paul knew this; in First Corinthians he wrote that "Christ has been raised from the dead, the firstfruits of those who have fallen asleep... in Christ all shall be brought to life, but each one in proper order: Christ the firstfruits; then at his coming, those who belong to Christ...."[48]

Well, we belong to Christ. And if we belong to Christ, we can look forward to a resurrection like his. The firstfruits were the first part of a crop to be harvested. It was brought to the temple as an offering, which led to the blessing of all the remaining harvest. And by his resurrection, Christ blesses us. He was the firstfruits; we will be part of the remaining harvest.

---

[48] 1 Corinthians 15:20, 22b-23.

Right now, living in this time between his Resurrection and ours, waiting on the final harvest, we form the Church. And in our worship and prayers, we're often reminded of the truth of the resurrection. When we recite the creed, we're reminded that the Church has always taught the resurrection of the body – not just a promise that we will live forever as spirits, but that we will have new bodies, like Jesus did. The Eucharist itself is a reminder that, just as bread and wine become the Body and Blood of Jesus, so our bodies will be transformed to be like Jesus. And when they are, we won't simply turn into ghosts, because a ghost does not have flesh and blood.

In one episode of *Casper the Friendly Ghost*, white cartoon ghosts are shown rising up out of graves in a spooky graveyard and flying away to scare people. But the graves remained closed, with coffins and bodies still in the graves. That is not what happened to Jesus, and despite what we might see or hear in cartoons or elsewhere, that's not what will happen to us.

When he appeared and his disciples were scared, Jesus said, "Why are you troubled?" He didn't want them to be scared, and he doesn't want us to be afraid either, not when we look at him now, or when we look forward to our own futures. His resurrection is a model for ours, and on the first Easter morning, his body was not in his tomb. He was a resurrected man, not a ghost, and we don't need to be afraid, because a ghost does not have flesh and blood.

Jesus lived and died a man. After his Resurrection, he was not a ghost. He was still a man, but he was changed. We live and die as humans. After our resurrection, we will not be ghosts. We will still be human but will be changed. The Gospel is the story of Jesus. And the Gospel is not a ghost story. Because a ghost does not have flesh and blood.

WHAT CAN YOU DO?
John 6:30-35

Tuesday of the Third Week of Easter, 21 Apr 2015

Many of us have been to a concert, or a sporting event, or perhaps a play, and seen what talented people can do. It's a pleasure to see talented people perform, and it's good to acknowledge their abilities. But when we see a musician or an athlete or an actor perform, that doesn't really tell us about their personality. It doesn't mean that, because we have seen them perform, we are suddenly their friend. We've seen that they can do, but that doesn't mean we really know who they are. Sometimes when we hear about one of these character's personal lives, we realize that perhaps they are not such a nice person, regardless of how talented they are, or what they can do.

In today's Gospel, people asked Jesus, "What can you do?" They wanted to know if he could do what they said Moses did – give them bread from heaven. But they are giving Moses credit for something God did – a mistake that Jesus corrected. And then Jesus challenged them to change their attitudes. He told them, "I am the bread of life." He challenged them to accept him for who he was – and not just for what he could do for them. If they did, they could enter a relationship that would last longer, and fulfill their hunger in a more profound way, than any physical bread ever would.

We know it's not healthy to value someone only for what they can do for us. Jesus invited the people he encountered into a relationship with him based on who he was and who they were. He does the same thing for us. He wants us to appreciate the wonderful and immeasurable things he does, but he also invites us to appreciate who he is and love him for that.

I think many of us would agree that we are trying to accept Jesus for who he is, and not just what he does. That doesn't mean that it's wrong to ask him for help. That's part of honest prayer. But it can be good for us to remember this gospel and ask ourselves if our balance is correct. While we often ask Jesus for our bread – do we too often forget that he is the Bread of Life?

SHEEP JOKES
John 19:27, Psalm 100:3

Fourth Sunday of Easter, 17 Apr 2016

At every Mass we hear Jesus called the Lamb of God. The priest says, "Behold the Lamb of God who takes away the sins of the world...." And in today's second reading, we hear Jesus called a Lamb.

But in that same reading, Jesus is also called a shepherd, and in the gospel, Jesus speaks as a shepherd, saying "my sheep hear my voice." And the psalm says that we are the sheep of his flock. So Jesus is seen as both the Lamb of God and the shepherd of his sheep. But we... are just sheep.

What does it mean to think about ourselves as sheep? You've probably heard homilies before that talk about how sheep need shepherds, how sheep are smelly, and aren't too smart, and so on. And there's plenty of evidence that sheep aren't very smart.

I recently heard a story about two sheep that were walking together in a field when they both fell into the same hole. One sheep started yelling, "baa! baa!" But the second sheep was quiet. And the first sheep yelled even louder, "baa! baa!" Then finally after a little while the second sheep said, "maybe we should yell together?" And the first sheep said, "together! together!"

So sheep have a reputation for not being very smart. I even heard the other day that a sheep actually got arrested for doing something dumb. It made an illegal ewe turn.

These jokes (lame as they are) might be a better picture of us as Christians than we like to admit. We're all part of a flock that sometimes takes wrong turns. And sometimes we find ourselves in a hole together, yelling for help. And even if we don't know exactly what to yell, Jesus is our shepherd who can help us out.

I've sometimes thought that I would personally be more comfortable if we were called sheep dogs instead of sheep. Dogs are smart, and sheep dogs are very smart. I heard about one farmer who sent his sheep dog out one evening to bring in the sheep, and when he came back the farmer said, "well, did you count them?" and the dog said, "yeah, there were 40 sheep." And the farmer said "40?? there were only 38 this morning!" and the dog said, "well, you did say to round them up."

I'm sorry... these are the best jokes sheep jokes I could find that were appropriate for a homily. But I've included them because I think jokes can remind us that sheep can be funny. And remembering that can be helpful. Because if we're sheep, which the Bible says we are, maybe sometimes we need a reminder not to take ourselves too seriously. Maybe we need to laugh at ourselves – in a healthy way – more than we do.

There is a serious side to being a sheep, which I will mention in just a minute. But there's a problem if we take ourselves too seriously and start thinking that we're smart enough that we can do fine all by ourselves, and that we don't need a shepherd.

Of course, all sheep aren't the same, and we're not all the same, either. That in itself can be a source of humor. Some of us are noisy, while some of us are quiet. And what do you call a quiet sheep, by the way? A sssshhhhhheeep. Some of us sit on the sidelines, while the others are dancing. And what do you call a dancing sheep? A baaaaalerina.

But to be serious – what are sheep for? To give wool and milk. To be killed and eaten. And in Biblical times, to be sacrificed. That doesn't sound so funny, does it? It's not. But to be a sacrifice doesn't require a lot of smarts, either. But for us, it does take being willing. Because one thing we do have that makes us different from sheep is free will. When it comes to being a sacrifice, we can say no. This might happen if we get the idea that we're too smart to follow the shepherd.

Talking about sacrifice might make us uneasy, but that's what sheep are for. We're called to follow our shepherd, Jesus, and become living sacrifices. When we follow him, we know we're in the right place to do that. And we have problems when we follow our own ideas, or the other sheep, and don't follow him.

Which reminds me: how many sheep does it take to change a light bulb? It takes 21 sheep. One sheep to take out the old light bulb, and 20 sheep to follow the first sheep around while he looks for a new one.

It's another dumb sheep joke... but aren't we like that sometimes? Isn't it easy to follow all the other sheep instead of following the Shepherd? But if we follow the other sheep, one day we might end up running off a cliff. And by the way – why did the ram run off the cliff? Because... he didn't see the ewe turn.

I know I'm not a comedian. But sheep can be funny, and sometimes we can be funny. And sometimes taking ourselves a little less seriously can help us remember that we need a shepherd. We're his property: we're the sheep of his flock. Our lives are ultimately his to use – he's the one who really knows where we should be going. If we want to resist that idea, because we take ourselves and our plans too seriously – maybe laughing at ourselves will help us remember.

Jesus, our shepherd, is both human and divine. He knows what it's like to hurt the way we hurt, because of his own human body. We might say that he lived in a sheep's body, like us, and that he died as the ultimate sacrifice. And that's one reason it makes sense to call our shepherd a Lamb.

So when Jesus asks us to give up our lives, to become sacrifices, he understands what he's asking. He's not asking us to do anything he hasn't already done himself. The Lamb of God died for us, and now he asks us to die for him.

JESUS OUR SHEPHERD
John 10:22

Tuesday of the Fourth Week of Easter, 19 Apr 2016

If today's gospel seems familiar, that might be because it includes our gospel from last Sunday, which we call Good Shepherd Sunday. But today's gospel begins at an earlier point in the story, where the specific time of year is mentioned: in winter, during the Feast of the Dedication. And we might wonder why we're told so carefully exactly when Jesus said these things about being the Good Shepherd.

The Feast of the Dedication is also called Hanukkah. It normally occurs during December. This gospel passage is the first place Hanukkah is mentioned in literature, and the only place it's mentioned in the Bible. During the celebration of the Feast of the Dedication, Ezekiel chapter 34 was read to the people. This is an entire chapter based on images of sheep and shepherds. Through the prophet, God told his people he would take away the shepherds of Israel who had failed to care for their sheep – in other words, their religious leaders. Instead, God says, "I myself will look after and tend my sheep. As a shepherd tends his flock when he finds himself among the scattered sheep, so will I tend my sheep."

Because it was Hanukkah, the religious leaders Jesus was talking to would have just been contemplating these words from their own prophet when Jesus said to them, "My sheep hear my voice: I know them, and they follow me." Jesus was describing himself in terms that God used in the prophetic books to describe himself. Jesus was claiming to be the true shepherd, and to be the replacement for the false shepherds, and doing it in a very timely way.

Sometimes people ask whether Jesus ever claimed to be God. He did, but as far as the gospels tell us he didn't simply say, "I'm God." He made his claim to be God in a way that was culturally relevant to the people he was talking to. He used the time of year, the places he visited, and other things as context, so people knew that he was not just claiming to be a God, or even the only God, but their God. His claim to be a shepherd was one of these claims. It wasn't a new image; it was one the people associated with their God already – one he had given them.

Jesus was the good shepherd of the people of Israel, and he's our good shepherd. Like the people in the gospels, we still live in a time and place where we see examples of poor leadership – in business, in government, and in Church. It's always good for us to be assured that we have a good shepherd to follow, who is Jesus, who is God.

PEACE I LEAVE YOU
John 14:27

Tuesday of the Fifth Week of Easter, 5 May 2015

Sooner or later, most of us find ourselves with someone who's struggling through a difficult moment in their life, perhaps even facing the end of their life. Some of us – counselors, pastors, nurses, hospice workers, and others – find ourselves in such situations frequently.

Often what matters at a time like this is just being with someone – what has sometimes been called the ministry of presence. Even if we can't do anything to fix what's wrong, we can still be with someone as they face it, and just being there – not as a problem solver, but simply as a companion – is the basis of the ministry of presence. And if we can comfort each other just by being with each other, we might imagine how Jesus could do the same if he could be with us. The good news is that he can. He is present when we are present to one another. And Jesus can also minister to us when we experience his presence in the Eucharist.

In every Mass we hear the priest say, "Peace I leave you; my peace I give you." These words come from John's gospel; in the reading we hear today. Just after he said this, Jesus reminded those with him that he had already told them, "I am going away, and I will come back to you." How did he leave us his peace? And how did he come back? Two ways were in his Church, and in the Eucharist.

It's sad and ironic that Christians don't always agree on what the Eucharist means, because the Real Presence of Jesus in the Eucharist is not meant to be a source of conflict – it's meant to be a source of comfort. Because he gave us the Church, and the Eucharist which we receive through the Church, Jesus can be with us whenever we need a comforting presence, and he will be with us until he comes again in another form.

NO UFO
Acts 1:11

Ascension of the Lord, 17 May 2015

One of my grad school professors[49] was a well-known expert on birds, especially the classification and naming of birds. But once I got to know him, I found out he was interested in a lot more than just birds. He loved basketball, for example, and would sometimes play pickup games with students less than half his age. He had been a Navy pilot during the years after World War II. And eventually I learned that he was recognized as an expert on UFOs – unidentified flying objects.

Now I thought of my professor as a serious scientist, and UFO investigation is not usually thought of as serious science, so I wondered about this, until finally one day I got the nerve to ask him how he had become interested in UFOs. And he told me a story.

He said that one day, when he was in pilot training, the officers took all the new pilots into a room and shut the door. And one of the officers said, "Today our topic is UFOs. There is no such thing as a UFO. And if you see one, here's what you do." And then the officers gave them detailed instructions to follow if they saw a UFO. And my professor said that since then, he'd always wondered why they gave him such careful instructions about what to do when he saw something that didn't exist.

I've never seen a UFO, unless you count birds that flew away before I could identify them, in which case I've seen thousands, and I have spent a lot of time watching the sky. Today, we're celebrating a unique event, when people watching the sky saw something they had never seen before, and who received instructions to follow once they did see this something in the sky. But this is not a story about a UFO.

Today we celebrate the Ascension, when Jesus left earth and rose through the sky to heaven, where he lives today. And Jesus is certainly not an alien or a UFO. We know who he is, and the Ascension, and its connection to Easter, help us know Jesus better. Our celebration of the Ascension doesn't just

---

[49] Dr. Burt L. Monroe, Jr., chair of the Department of Life Sciences at the University of Louisville for 23 years, President of the American Ornithologists' Union (1990-92), prolific author, and good friend.

follow Easter on the calendar. It's also related to Easter in what it tells us about Jesus, and the instructions he left for us to follow.

The connection between Easter and the Ascension is made clear by the language of Acts, in the reading we've just heard. Remember that Luke wrote both the gospel that bears his name and the book of Acts. The Ascension had already been described by Luke at the end of his gospel, but at the beginning of Acts, he describes it again, with more details, details that make it clear that we should think of the Ascension together with the Resurrection.

Although we read about the Ascension in other places, only in the version in Acts do we read about the two men dressed in white who appear suddenly to the men of Galilee who were watching Jesus ascend to heaven. We understand these men in white to have been angels, but Luke doesn't use the word angel here. And when was the last time before this in the writings of Luke that two men dressed in bright clothing had suddenly appeared to the followers of Jesus? On the first Easter morning, when the women of Galilee came to the tomb of Jesus and found it empty: the gospel says, two men in dazzling garments appeared to them.

Now, at the Ascension, two men in white appear again. On the first Easter morning these men, or angels, had asked, "Why do you seek the living one among the dead?" Now they ask, "why are you standing there looking at the sky?" The women were sent from the tomb to tell his followers the Good News; now his followers were sent to tell the world the Good News.

Jesus told his disciples to wait for the coming of the Holy Spirit, and then, after that experience, to go through the whole world and tell the good news about him. We sometimes call these instructions the Great Commission. The early Church followed these instructions; they went out and turned the world upside down, as it says later in Acts, telling people about Jesus, baptizing them, offering the presence of Jesus in the Eucharist, and building the Church.

We are part of that same Church – the Church that knows Jesus is alive, that knows the outpouring of the Holy Spirit, that went out and turned the world upside down, that sometimes still turns the world upside down, energized by the reality of the Resurrection and the Ascension.

The followers of Jesus had spent 40 days after his Resurrection with him. They knew he was real. Different, but real. They knew who they were watching when he ascended into heaven; he was no UFO. Today, we still know who he is. Despite the confusing messages we sometimes hear from outside the Church, he is not unidentified, flying or otherwise. Jesus is God, Messiah, Christ, and Savior, fully human and fully divine, and he is as real today as he has always been. He sends us his Spirit, as he promised he would, and he comes to us in the Eucharist, as he has done since the earliest days of the Church.

Jesus was raised from the tomb; he was also raised into heaven. We don't need to stand here, looking at the sky, wondering what we're looking at, or who we're looking for. Jesus is in heaven, but he's not a UFO, and we don't see him in the sky, we see him here, in the Church. We come here and see Jesus, and we have a set of instructions to follow, the same instructions given to the Church after the first Easter and the Ascension. Seek the Holy Spirit and go tell people about him. Start at home and reach the whole world.

FEEL THE BURN
Acts 2:3

Pentecost Sunday, 15 May 2016

What happens when a small, privileged group of men gets control of a government? Can such a group ever resist the temptation to use the resources of the people for their personal benefit, rather than for the good of everyone? Can they stay true to the mission of the founders of that government? Can they tell the truth as it really is, instead of as they want it to be? There's one way to make sure that a small group like that does not abuse their position. And that's to be sure those leaders feel the burn.[50]

Now in case you're wondering – I'm not talking about the United States of America. I'm talking about a government that's about 2000 years old, and the small group of men who were put in charge of that government, and whose successors still lead that government. I'm talking about the apostles, and the bishops, and the Catholic Church they still lead. Jesus left the apostles to govern our Church. And the first thing they did was to wait together, and pray together, until the time came for them to feel the burn. Or, as it says in chapter 2 of the book of Acts, after they had been praying together, "tongues as of fire... came to rest on each one of them." And when this happened, they were filled with God's Spirit.

But today, I'm not just talking about the apostles – I'm also talking about us – and how we need to feel the burn, just like they did. God called the apostles – they prayed together until they felt the burn – and then they got to work. And that's a pattern we should see in our lives as well.

Have you ever been burned? I don't mean metaphorically – I mean literally. If you've ever touched a hot stove, or a hot curling iron, or put food in your mouth that was too hot, you know that being burned can hurt. It can even be deadly. The effects of feeling the burn can last for minutes, or days, or can even leave a permanent scar. Fire can hurt, and kill, and destroy.

But when it's kept under control, feeling the burn is a good thing. When it's cold outside, we can burn things to stay warm. Most of us burned gasoline in

---

[50] This phrase was being used by the campaign of Bernie Sanders, who was running for the Democratic nomination for president at the time this was preached. I had fun using it to get people's attention and then repurposing it.

our cars to get here this morning. When we cook, we use the heat to make sure our food is safe to eat. So burning isn't always dangerous – it can also be helpful and purifying. And in our Church, and in our lives, burning should be a good thing, if the burn we feel is the fire of the Holy Spirit, like it was for the apostles.

God's power is unlimited. If he wanted to burn us up, and get rid of us, he could. But instead, he sends the fire of his spirit to mature us, to purify us, and to empower us. When we feel the burn of the Holy Spirit, we're not feeling the full power of God – we couldn't stand it. But God will send us just the right amount of heat to get us ready for the job he has for us to do.

Sometimes we might say our spiritual life is like cooking: we have half-baked ideas about our faith, or about what God wants us to do, and God needs to heat things up a little bit in our lives to help us grow, and to make sure we end up well-done. Those of you who cook know we don't cook everything on the highest heat setting on the stove; sometimes it's better just to simmer things and cook them gradually. And sometimes our lives are like that, too. We need to cook slowly, with the Holy Spirit working on us gently, to get us where he wants us to be.

But – there are other times! When the apostles felt the burn of the tongues of flame, that was one of those times when the heat was turned up pretty high. Because God knew he was starting a fire that would still be keeping us warm 2000 years later.

When we read that story of the apostles being together in the upper room, and feeling the burn of the Holy Spirit – we can remember that it hadn't been very long since they were running in fear while Jesus was arrested, and not very long since they were hiding while he was being crucified.

And even though they'd been with Jesus after His Resurrection, we know the apostles still had some things to learn. They were still at least a little half-baked, like some of us. But we also know that God took them the way they were and sent them out to spread the good news about Jesus. He told them to wait for the Holy Spirit before they went – but once they felt the burn, they were ready to go. And he does that with us, too.

Every one of us here today has a vocation – some plan God has for us, individually, something he's asking us to do. The apostles were called to govern the Church at its very beginning. We're not. But we are called to many other things. And like the apostles, we need to feel the burn of the Holy Spirit to do whatever God has for us to do. And because we're part of this Church that has been led by the Holy Spirit for nearly 2000 years, and because of the sacraments, and because of the promise of Jesus that he would send his spirit to guide his followers, we know we can feel the burn.

We shouldn't make the mistake of thinking that when we feel the burn it will be just like it was for the apostles. We're not them. We don't live in the same circumstances they do. When you or I feel the burn it's usually not quite so dramatic. For us, it might be the gentle warmth of a friend, or a casual suggestion that comes from a family member. It might be what we feel when we receive the Eucharist, which is after all, the body and blood of the one whose Spirit is doing the burning.

Now, one of these days, for some of us – feeling the burn of the Holy Spirit might mean a roaring wind, and a burning flame, and a sudden ability to speak another language. We can't limit God. Most of the time, for most of us, it won't be like that, but one way or another, we can all expect to feel the burn if we're listening to God, and asking him what our vocation is, and what we should do next in our lives.

I have no idea who our next president will be. I have no idea who our next pope will be. But I do know that God gave us the apostles and their successors to lead his Church, and that we're part of that Church. And Jesus promised that he would send his Spirit to guide us, and he did. Because he made this promise, and because he's been keeping his promise for 2000 years, we know that when we need it, just like the apostles, we can feel the burn.

One winter night, when I was about 14, my mother woke me up in the middle of the night and told me that a house just down the street was on fire. I jumped out of bed and went to see, and as I walked out of my house and looked down the road, I realized that even though that other house was out of sight down the hill, I could see the glow from the fire against the night sky. I ran down the road until I reached the driveway to that house. It sat back about 200 yards off the street. And as I stood there by the mailbox and watched that house burn, I realized that even though it was that far away, I could feel the heat from that fire. And although there were firemen there, trying to control the fire, by the next morning, the house was gone.

Our question today is whether our lives, and this Church, here in Scottsville and around the world, will be like that house on fire. One day we'll be gone. But right now, can people see the glow from our fire? Can people feel the heat we give off, even if they aren't here with us? God is calling us to light up the sky for the world; he's calling us to bring his warmth into dark places; he's calling us to feel the burn.

SAINTS

BEING A MOTHER
Luke 2:19

Solemnity of the Blessed Virgin Mary, the Mother of God,
1 Jan 2015
Holy Name of Mary, Bedford, VA

What does a Mother do? She helps her child to grow. First, her child grows within her. Then her child is born. And then she encourages her child to keep growing, and she introduces him to others.

Like any mother, Mary remembered the events surrounding the birth of her child; the gospel says "she kept all these things, reflecting on them in her heart." These events showed the unique nature of her child. A human baby, but also God, come to earth in human form.

Like any saint, Mary is an example for us, a model for us. But Mary is unique – not just a saint, but the only sinless saint, and the one-of-a-kind mother of God. We look to the saints as models for our lives. But – how could any of us be the mother of God?

Mary allowed Jesus to grow within her. Can we do this? Yes. We can, and we should. How does Jesus come to live within us? Through encounters with his living Church. Through reading his word, and hearing it proclaimed. Most of all, through receiving Him when we receive the Holy Eucharist.

Mary gave birth to Jesus, then showed him to others. Can we do this? Yes. We can, and we should. We show Jesus to others in our words, and in our actions. We show Jesus to others by how we treat them. Are we merciful? Are we forgiving? Are we thankful to God and to others? Do we tell the truth, even when it hurts us to do so? As a Church, how do we treat the poor, the abandoned, and the abused? If we treat them as Jesus did – by helping and welcoming them – then we show Jesus to others.

Mary encouraged Jesus to keep growing. Can we do this? Yes. We can, and we should. Mary had the unique privilege of helping Jesus grow from a baby into a boy and then into a man. Jesus is God, and of course he is complete and perfect. But we can help his presence – the awareness of his Holy Spirit – grow in the lives of others. We can help his presence grow in our community. We can help his presence grow in our nation, and in our world.

Mary nurtured Jesus, before and after his birth, and helped him live the life God called him to. She was the ideal mother. And she did all this without sin. And are we called to do this? Yes. None of us reaches the level of perfection she attained. But that's our goal. To become saints ourselves. And it's Jesus himself who makes this possible, who offers us forgiveness for our sins, who can help us share him with others, who can make us more like his mother.

How do we do all this? With the help of Jesus, how do we follow the example of Mary, the woman we celebrate today as the Mother of God? The gospel tells us. Mary shows us. And our actions at every Mass help us. Our celebration of the motherhood of Mary is a celebration, but it can also be a challenge to us. The good news is that Mary, and most of all her son, want us to be like them, and will help us to be like them.

Be like Mary. Let Jesus grow inside you. Reflect on what Jesus does for you. And show him to everyone you meet.

DISTRACTED DRIVERS
Luke 2:19

Solemnity of the Blessed Virgin Mary, the Mother of God,
1 Jan 2016
Holy Name of Mary, Bedford, VA

I'm a teacher, and one morning a few weeks ago, I was driving to school, and my son Jeremy was in the car with me. As we got to a long curve in the highway, I noticed a car that was coming the other way was drifting across the yellow line, moving into my lane. I moved over slightly and assumed he would move back into his lane – but he didn't. He kept drifting over towards me, and I moved over some more, and he kept coming, until finally at the last second I jerked my wheel to the right – then there was a loud "bang!" and then what was left of my rear view mirror was dangling from a wire, thumping the side of my car door, as I drove on down the road.

I called the police, and they caught the guy a few miles up the road, and now his insurance company and mine are working out the details. But then, later that day, I suddenly realized – I could have been dead! The guy in the other car was obviously distracted. If I'd also been distracted and hadn't swerved at the last second, we would have hit head on, and Jeremy and I could have both been killed.

Now this isn't just a homily against distracted driving, even though I'm more concerned about it now than ever. But it is about distraction in a more general sense, and I do want to emphasize that distraction can be deadly – not just physically, but also spiritually. You might have heard discussions recently about how in our society we're constantly distracted – not just when we're driving, but all the time. I know that it's a constant problem for me to keep my students' attention. I don't allow cell phones to be used in my classes, but my students still try to use them – even though the penalty when they do is a zero on an assignment.

And I see this in Church, too. Several weeks ago, I was at Mass in a parish in another state and the man down the pew from me was distracting me – by checking his cell phone in the middle of Mass, both during the homily and during the Eucharistic Prayer.

OK, I'm intentionally NOT looking around right now to see if anyone is putting away their cell phone....

But the problem isn't just smart phones. It's also television and laptops and iPads and all kinds of other entertainment devices. And it's not just technology. It's also busy schedules, and the demands of school and jobs, and difficult personal situations, and the inability to say no. All these things combine to distract us. And it's not just our relationships with each other that are messed up. We're also distracted from Jesus. And being distracted from Jesus, our source of truth, our source of peace, can be as deadly to us spiritually, as a head-on collision can be physically. So how can we avoid it?

Even if we're not literally driving, we are all traveling down the road of our lives. And as we start the new year, this might be a good time to ask for help from someone who's an ideal model of what it means not to be distracted from the things that really matter – and that's Mary, the Mother of God, whom we celebrate today.

Today's gospel says that after the birth of Jesus, and the appearance of the angels, and the visit from the shepherds, "Mary kept all these things, reflecting on them in her heart." Some translations say she was pondering these things in her heart. What was she pondering? The wonderful things about this new baby, Jesus. Who he was, what he meant to her, and what he meant to the world?

We know that Jesus is God, so we can honor Mary as we do today as the Mother of God. And she is also our Mother. And as Mother of God, and our mother, she's an ideal source of help when we're spiritually distracted. Mary's attitude towards Jesus – her reflection, her pondering – is the opposite of spiritual distraction.

The gospels make a point of presenting Mary to us as a model for our lives. In the same chapter as our gospel reading, Luke 2 – after Mary and Joseph find the boy Jesus in the temple – we're told again, "his mother kept all these things in her heart." So we see Mary as a model of someone who was not distracted from what really matters. Mary kept these things in her heart and pondered them – and so should we.

So Mary is a model – but she's also something more than a model. She's not just someone from the past who we remember, someone who once upon a time managed to live an ideal spiritual life. She's also our help today as we try to follow her model. We don't just try to be like Mary; we ask Mary to help us be like her. We don't just admire her lack of distraction – we ask her to help with our distraction. And she will help us, just as she's been helping Christians for nearly 2000 years.

How do we ask her for help? Prayer is the obvious answer. Of course that includes the rosary, and Marian prayers such as the Memo rare, but it also includes spontaneous prayer. We can pray to Mary anywhere, anytime, in any words that say what we really feel. The type of prayer that can work even in a busy, distracted lifestyle. Mary is the Mother of God, but she's also our mother. And she listens to us the way a loving mother listens to her children. Our words don't have to be perfect. We can say just what we feel. When we talk to Mary and tell her that the distractions in our life are keeping us from focusing on her son, she will help us.

In just a few minutes many of us are going to be driving home. So, don't look at your phones while you're driving, OK. But whether we're walking, or riding, or driving, all of us this morning is traveling into 2016. We're all at the beginning of this journey through another year in our lives. And when it comes to our spiritual life – our relationship with Jesus – we have a chance to decide whether we'll be distracted drivers, or whether we'll ask Mary to help us be more like her – to take the time we need to reflect on her Son in our hearts.

BLAISE, THE HOLY HELPER
Hebrews 12:1

Memorial of Saint Blaise, 3 Feb 2015

One September day more than 550 years ago, a Bavarian shepherd was watching his sheep when he saw a small child sitting in the middle of a field, alone and crying. He walked over to the child, intending to pick it up, but just as he reached it – the child disappeared. Not long after that, he saw the child again, but this time, near the child, he also saw two lighted candles. Again he approached the child – and again it disappeared.

The next summer, the shepherd was in the same area, and one day he saw the child again. This time, when he approached, he saw 13 other small children with the first. He also saw that the first child had a red cross on its chest. When he got closer, the child spoke to him, and said, "We are the 14 helpers. We wish for a chapel to be built here. If you will serve us, we will serve you."

The shepherd knew who the 14 helpers were: 14 saints who were honored together in the medieval Church, especially in Germany. The field belonged to a group of Cistercian monks, and when they heard the shepherd's story, the Cistercians built a chapel in honor of the 14 holy helpers. Worship began there in 1448, and the site has been a destination for pilgrims since. In the 18th century, a large Church was built there that's still present today, the Basilica of the Fourteen Holy Helpers.

Today's reading from Hebrews assured the early Christians that they were surrounded by "a cloud of witnesses," great figures from the Old Testament such as Abraham and Sarah, Isaac, Joseph, Moses, David, Samuel, and others who had been named in the preceding verses. We're fortunate to look back to the examples of these Old Testament characters, as well as a long list of saints from nearly 2000 years of Christian history. Among them would be the 14 helpers honored in that basilica in Bavaria, and among those 14 is one whose feast we celebrate today: Saint Blaise.

Saint Blaise was from the part of the world we know as central Turkey. He's said to have been a doctor before becoming the Bishop of Sebastea. This was in the early third century, during a time of persecution for the Church, and when Blaise came into conflict with the Roman governor, he was captured and imprisoned. As Blaise was being led to prison, a woman rushed up with her only son who was choking on a fish bone. Or perhaps she rushed to see

Blaise after he had been imprisoned – versions of the story differ. But the stories say that either by touching the holy bishop, or through his prayers, the boy was saved.

A short time later, Blaise was tortured and executed by the governor when he would not renounce his faith. The people remembered Blaise and began to pray to him. He became recognized as a saint to whom one prayed for help with throat ailments of any kind, and the earliest known reference to him makes this association. Throat ailments are common, and Blaise has remained popular for centuries.

We don't know if all the details in all the stories about Blaise are true; the ancient world's understanding of history is not ours.[51] And we don't know if the story about the 14 children appearing on the hillside in Bavaria is true; the medieval world's understanding of history is not ours. But we do know that the Church encourages our prayers to Blaise, and to all of the thousands of recognized saints who form a "cloud of witnesses."[52] They are models for us and remain willing to help us through their prayers.

---

[51] For more stories about Blaise and a brief but responsible consideration of his life, see *Butler's Lives of the Saints, New Full Edition*, February volume, 1998, Burns & Oates/The Liturgical Press, pp. 34-35.
[52] *CCC*, 2683.

BEING WHERE YOU'RE MEANT TO BE
Mark 16:15

Memorial of Saint Patrick, 17 Mar 2015

Saint Patrick, whose feast we celebrate today, is one of the patron saints of Ireland. He's so closely associated with Ireland that we often overlook a basic fact about him: he was not Irish.

Patrick was a Roman Briton who was captured by slave traders as a young man and taken to Ireland as a slave. He eventually escaped but went back to Ireland as a Christian missionary and bishop years later. We know this because we're blessed to have two works that he wrote himself, including his *Confession*. Patrick's *Confession* gives us many details about his life. Although Patrick was not Irish by birth, he deserves much of the credit, humanly speaking, for bringing Christianity to Ireland.

If you had been a slave, and then escaped, you might think it was crazy to ever consider going back to the place you escaped from. But that's what God called Patrick to do, and that's what Patrick did. The irony is that Patrick's enslavement in a way led to freedom for his enslavers.

In his *Confession*, Patrick says honestly that if he thought it was the right thing to do, he "would have been only too ready... to see my own country once more, and my parents..." and "...also to cross over to Gaul and visit my brothers there... God knows only too well how much I longed for that...."[53] But he didn't not feel free to leave Ireland, and so added a few lines later that he planned to "be with [the Irish] for the rest of my life, if the Lord so desires."

Patrick is not the only saint we often identify with their place of ministry rather than their place of origin. Two more recent examples are Mother Teresa in India, and Saint Damien in Hawaii. Do you know where they were from originally?[54]

Patrick's story can be a useful reminder to us. In the lives of Patrick and other saints, what was most important was doing what God called them to do and

---

[53] *Confession*, section 43. My quotations are from *The Confession of St. Patrick* and *Letter to Coroticus*, translated by John Skinner, 1998, Image/ Doubleday.
[54] Mother Teresa was from what is now North Macedonia, formerly part of Yugoslavia, formerly in the Ottoman Empire; Father Damian was from Belgium.

being where God called them to be. Life should be that way for us. We might be called to serve God in the very place we're from – or it might be the ends of the earth, which is where Patrick thought Ireland was.[55] And we might get there traveling routes that are comfortable and predictable – but, like Saint Patrick, we might not.

---

[55] Patrick makes comments to this effect in his *Confession*; see sections 1 and 34. See also, for example, the discussion in *St. Patrick of Ireland: A Biography*, by Philip Freeman, 2004, Simon & Schuster, chapter 10.

PHILIP AND JAMES AND ALL THE REST
John 14:8-9

Feast of Saints Philip and James, 3 May 2016

Some questions are hard to answer. And one of those questions is, "How many Churches are there in Rome?" Some sources say more than 600, some say more than 900. Among other things, it depends on where you draw the line around what you consider Rome, and it depends on what counts as a separate Church.

A few years ago I was in Rome with my son Cassidy and we visited one of those hundreds of Churches, the Church dedicated to the apostle Bartholomew.[56] After we visited that Church and venerated the relics there, I began to wonder: where are the other major Churches devoted to the 12 apostles, where their relics are venerated? I knew St Peter was at St Peter's, of course, and I remembered that St James the Great was in Santiago de Compostela in Spain, and now I knew where Bartholomew was, but that still left more than half of the 12.

After looking around I discovered that there was a Church there in Rome devoted to all 12 apostles, and we decided to visit.[57] But when we went there, we discovered that the Church had an older name. Ever since the rule of Pope John III (not Twenty-third... Third... in the sixth century...) it had been called the Church of St. Philip and St. James until the name was changed to honor all the apostles. And the feast day associated with that Church, and those two disciples, is the feast we celebrate today.

But why Philip and James together? and, to be clear, which James? Because two of the 12 apostles were named James. We don't know a lot about these two apostles. Though we do know both were together when Jesus worked many miracles, at the Last Supper, and at Pentecost.

Philip was the apostle at the Last Supper who said to Jesus, "Show us the Father," which led Jesus to respond, whoever has seen me has seen the Father. Philip was also involved in one of the stories of the miraculous

---

[56] The Basilica di San Bartolomeo all'Isola, located on Tiber Island. It contains relics of many 20th and 21st century saints as well as of St. Bartholomew.

[57] Usually known as Santi Apostoli, the original building was destroyed by an earthquake in 1348, but was rebuilt in the following century and has been renovated a few times since.

feeding of 5000 people. The James who is honored with Philip is the apostle called James the Less, or James the Minor, who is not the one associated with the famous Church of Santiago de Compostela in Spain or who was at the Transfiguration with Jesus – that was James the Great. In fact, there are about six or eight Jameses in the New Testament and it's sometimes hard to figure out which one the text is talking about. But the James we honor today was the James who led the early Church in Jerusalem, as described in the book of Acts.

Why a single Church was built to house the relics of these apostles together isn't clear, but a few observations can be made. We do at least know their names – and Philip is a Greek name, while James is equivalent to Jacob, a Hebrew name. So putting them together represents bringing together the two parts of the early Church, the Gentiles and the Jews, which had to be brought together to ensure the survival and spread of Christianity.

Both of these apostles were also martyred for their faith, and in particular for their leadership in the early Church, and so we wear red, the color of blood.[58] The stories say that Philip was crucified, while James was clubbed to death. And James remained in Jerusalem while Philip was spreading the gospel in what is today Turkey, so in that way also they represent two strands of growth in the early Church.

So Philip and James are witnesses to us of how different members of our Church should work together, while we're also finding our own particular path as we follow Jesus. These apostles are witnesses to us, as were most of the apostles, of being willing to die for our faith. They ended up in the same place – not just in the Church of the Holy Apostles in Rome, but in heaven. And no matter where we end up in this life, I hope we will profit by their example and their prayers, and after this life, end up with them in heaven.

---

[58] A reference to the fact that on this day, as on other feast days honoring martyrs, Catholic clergy wear red vestments.

SEEING CLEARLY
Tobit 2:9-14

Memorial of Saints Marcellinus and Peter, 2 June 2015

How could a deacon who is also an ornithologist pass up a chance to preach about bird droppings?

We heard part of Tobit's story in the first reading, in which he blames bird droppings for giving him cataracts. The story is not meant to be science, and we shouldn't judge it by scientific standards. No, cataracts are not caused by bird poop. But Tobit, who is telling this story, thought they were. This isn't modern medicine, but it is a good story, and when we hear it, we remember Tobit's blindness because of how the story is told.

Tobit's blindness, and how he recovered his sight, can be important images for us. Physical blindness is often a metaphor for spiritual blindness, and the return of sight can be an image of spiritual awakening. For Tobit, the return of his vision led literally to a spiritual awakening after his sight was returned. His prayer, which follows the return of his sight, is heard in our Church's liturgy; it was our second reading in Morning Prayer this morning.

On this date, 2 June, the Church remembers two martyrs from the early 4th century, Marcellinus and Peter. They were beheaded together outside of Rome, but their remains were recovered, and a Church was to honor them. Stories say that they went willingly to their place of execution and sang while they cleared the brush from the piece of land where they were then killed and buried.

Hearing part of the story of Tobit, and then part of the story of Marcellinus and Peter, we might not see a connection at first. But Marcellinus and Peter are two great examples of saints who see clearly. They saw clearly the value of obeying God and following him faithfully, even though it cost their lives. Tobit's physical sight was returned, and this led to spiritual insight. The saints give us many examples of those with highly developed spiritual insight. And as Christians, we're called to seek the same spiritual insight that Tobit and the saints model for us.

Just today, 2 June, in addition to Sts. Marcellinus and Peter, the Church recognizes St. Erasmus of Formia, an early 4th-century bishop and martyr from Croatia; St Stephen of Sweden, an 11th-century bishop and martyr; and Blessed Sadok and his companions, a group of 49 Dominican martyrs who died in Poland in 1260. All of these martyrs also saw clearly. They saw that earthly status was not as important as spiritual status, that life on earth was meant to be a prelude to life in heaven, and that the most valuable vision is the beatific vision, the sight of God which we all pray we will attain.

JOHN VIANNEY'S RISKS
Matthew 14:22-33

Memorial of Saint John Vianney, 4 Aug 2015

When his disciples saw Jesus walking on the water, through the wind and waves, they were afraid. Jesus spoke to them and told them not to be afraid. But only Peter replied, and got out of the boat, and started walking towards Jesus. When Jesus spoke to him, Peter took a risk.

Today is the feast of St John Vianney. The French Revolution started when John Vianney was four years old. Suddenly the Catholic Church was illegal in this country that had a rich Catholic history. Priests were persecuted; Masses had to be said in secret. But John's family knew priests and arranged religious instruction for him. At his First Communion Mass, the windows were covered so no one would see the candles burning and know priests were there. Those priests, like the apostle Peter, took a risk.

As a young man, John Vianney wanted to be a priest, but faced many obstacles. In 1802 the Church became legal again, but Napoleon was in power, and was searching for soldiers. At times John had to hide in a barn, in piles of rotting hay, to avoid being forced into the army or arrested. He fell behind in his academic work. He was often sick. Despite all these hardships, he was ordained in 1815. To become a priest, John Vianney took a risk.

Vianney wished for a quiet life as a parish priest, but his skill as a pastor attracted thousands of pilgrims. Some days he spent 12 hours or more hearing confessions and counseling pilgrims who came to meet with him. He almost died due to serious illness but continued his busy schedule. John Vianney took a risk to remain a priest, until he died at age 73.

The Catholic Church might not be illegal in our country – not yet, at least. But every day our society gives us the opportunity to take a risk when we listen to Jesus, even if our risks are less than those taken by Peter, or the priests of the French Revolution, or St John Vianney.

It's a risk to stand for what marriage and families really are. It's a risk to defend the life of every unborn child. It's a risk to say that there are absolute truths that cannot be changed based on personal preference, or a vote. As Christians we're each called in our own way, in our own lives, to follow the examples of Peter, of John Vianney, and of many other saints – to take a risk.

MARY, US, AND THE ARCHANGELS
Tobit 3:16-17; Revelation 12:7-8; Luke 1:26-27

Feast of Saints Michael, Gabriel, and Raphael, Archangels,
29 Sept 2015

The Bible names three archangels – Raphael, Michael, and Gabriel – and tells fascinating stories about each. Raphael, in the book of Tobit, heals the blindness of Tobit, a righteous Israelite, and helps his son Tobiah meet and marry his wife Sarah. Michael, in the Revelation of John, leads the angels in battle against the enemies of God and defeats a dragon who is identified as Satan. And Gabriel, in the gospel of Luke, appears to Mary and announces that she will have a son, Jesus, who will be the ruler of his people forever.

As we celebrate the feast of the archangels, we could learn helpful lessons from any of these stories. I'd like to think a little longer about the meeting between Gabriel and Mary, which we often call the Annunciation. If we remember that Mary is a symbol of the Church, her response to Gabriel can help us think about how we should respond to the angels who surround us, and to the messages they carry.

First of all, Mary does not deny Gabriel's existence. It would be hard since he was standing there in front of her! Today, some people seem to live as though angels aren't real – maybe even some Catholics. But if we deny that angels exist, if we forget that they know us and are here with us, and might still be sent by God to interact with us, we really don't have a complete awareness of the world we live in.

Second, Mary listened to Gabriel's message. The message of an angel is a message from God. Angel means messenger, and we might expect the archangels to be sent with some of the most important messages. For Mary, this was definitely true – the message was the Good News that Jesus would be born and lead his people to new life. But if Mary had not listened, where would we be?

Third, Mary acted on what Gabriel told her – not just because he's an angel, but also because his message was the word of God. We might not routinely have face-to-face conversations with archangels, but we do read the word of God in our scriptures, and hear it proclaimed by our Church. So, how do we act on it? Mary left to go and visit Elizabeth based on what Gabriel told her. Does hearing the word of God cause us to change our plans?

Fourth, Mary spoke to Gabriel. She talked back – respectfully! She asked for clarification about what she was hearing. So how do we talk to the angels? We can, through prayer. If we follow Mary's example then we see that it's a good idea to talk to the angels, to ask them for help. And we can pray to them – in the familiar prayer to St. Michael, in prayer to our guardian angel, or in other ways.

In some ways the angels are like us. They're personal, and they're created by God. But they're also distinctly different from us. They don't routinely inhabit physical bodies – they're inherently spiritual. And they're intelligent in a way and to a degree that we can't understand. People are not angels and can never become angels. We aren't meant to be angels; we are meant to listen to them. On the feast of the archangels, Raphael, Michael, and Gabriel, we have a special opportunity to thank God for those three, and for all angels, and remember that they are part of the world God has given us, and in which we live our lives as Christians.

FRANCIS AND THE EUCHARIST
Galatians 6:17

Memorial of Saint Francis of Assisi, 4 Oct 2016

Francis of Assisi is one of the most popular and most recognized of all saints. Even many non-Catholics know who he is. People often recognize pictures of him, and statues like the one outside our Church, and many people know some of the stories about him.

One story tells how, when his father was upset with him, Francis stripped naked in front of the bishop and gave his father all his clothes. Another story tells how he talked to a wolf that was terrorizing a town and convinced it to stop attacking the people and their livestock. Another story, one I especially love, is that he preached to a large flock of birds that sat and listened to him until he blessed them and sent them away. And another story tells how he received the stigmata – wounds on his hands and feet and in his side that matched the wounds received by Jesus on the cross.

These stories are wonderful. But to go with them, we also have actual writings by Francis, and if we really want to get to know him, we don't have to limit ourselves to the stories other people told about him, as wonderful as they are. We can read his actual words.[59] And when I read what Francis himself wrote, I was struck by something that we sometimes don't hear in the stories about Francis, and that was how much he loved the Eucharist – the actual Body and Blood of Jesus.

In one letter, for example, Francis wrote, "I implore all of you brothers to show all possible reverence and honor to the most holy Body and Blood of our Lord Jesus Christ in Whom that which is in the heavens and on the earth is brought to peace and is reconciled to the all-powerful God."[60]

And in another letter, he wrote, "humbly beg the clergy to revere above everything else the most holy Body and Blood of our Lord Jesus Christ.... And when It is sacrificed upon the altar by the priest and carried to any place, let all the people, on bended knee, praise, glorify, and honor the Lord God

---

[59] Collected and translated in *Francis and Clare: The Complete Works*, by Regis J. Armstrong, O.F.M. CAP., and Ignatius C. Brady, O.F.M., 1982, Paulist Press, from which my quotations are taken.
[60] A Letter to the Entire Order, sections 12-13.

living and true."[61] And I could share many other similar quotes. Francis loved the Eucharist, and he begged others to respect the Body of Christ, as he did.

Like all saints, we can look to Francis as a model for our lives for many reasons: because he loved the natural world, because of his love for poverty, because of his ecumenical spirit – but let's not overlook this fundamental character that he himself wanted others to see in him: his love for the Eucharist.

If we're going to imitate Jesus by imitating Francis, we might not tame any wolves, and we might not get the birds to listen to our sermons, and I hope we don't end up stripping naked in front of the bishop – but we can and we should show love to the Body and Blood of Jesus Christ, just as he did.

---

[61] The First Letter to the Custodians, sections 2, 6.

LUKE'S STORIES
Luke 1:1-4

Feast of Saint Luke, Evangelist, 18 Oct 2016

Here's a list of stories:

- The story of the Annunciation, when the angel Gabriel told Mary, a young virgin, that she would have a son.

- The story of the priest Zachariah being made speechless by an angel when he doubted he would have a son, and the song he sang when his son was born, and his speech returned – a song the Church prays every day at Morning Prayer.

- The story of the Visitation, when Mary travels to spend several months with her cousin Elizabeth while both are pregnant, and the song she prayed on her arrival, the Magnificat – which the Church repeats every day in Evening Prayer.

- The story of Jesus being born in a stable, laid in a manger, and visited by shepherds.

- The story of the Prodigal Son, returning to his father in shame, only to be welcomed home.

- The story of Zacchaeus climbing a tree to see Jesus, and then being called down to have dinner with him.

- The story of Pentecost, when tongues of fire came from heaven, and the Church began to spread around the world.

- The story of Stephen, the first Christian martyr, being stoned to death.

Now here's a question: What do all these stories have in common?

And here's the answer: we know them all because of Luke, the evangelist. In our Bible, these stories are all found in the gospel of Luke or the book of Acts, which he wrote, and nowhere else. Although Paul wrote more separate titles, more of the words of the New Testament came from the pen of Luke than from any other writer.

Besides this inspired writing, Luke is said to have been a painter who made icons of the Blessed Virgin Mary, and to have been a doctor who accompanied Paul on many of his travels. It's also said that perhaps Luke knew the Blessed Virgin personally, and that he was martyred by being hung. So he has quite a resume, even if some of the things we hear about him might not be historically verifiable. He has clearly had a great influence on everyday Christianity.

Every time we pray Morning Prayer, Evening Prayer, the rosary, or tell the story of Baby Jesus in the manger.... we're using the words of Luke. It's good today, on his feast day, to thank God for him and his witness, and to ask him to pray for us as we try to be witnesses to the truth about Jesus in our own lives.

THE ONLY TRAGEDY
Matthew 5:1-12a

Solemnity of All Saints, 1 Nov 2016

All Saints' Day, when we remember ALL the saints that the Church has recognized, is also a good day to remember the answer to the question: what is a saint? We might say, saints are people who we know are in heaven. And we could also say, saints are holy people. And we can point to many examples to get an idea of what it looks like to live a holy life.

Mary is the first and greatest example of a saint, and there are thousands of others. They include martyrs of the early Church like Ignatius of Antioch, who was fed to the lions in Rome, as well as martyrs who have died in recent years. They include great theologians like Athanasius and Basil, and popes like Gregory the Great and John Paul II. Some founded religious orders, like St. Dominic, St. Francis, St. Ignatius of Loyola, and St. Teresa of Calcutta. Some, like our patron St. George, we don't know as much about as we would like. On some days we remember dozens of saints at once, such as the 118 Vietnamese Martyrs we'll honor later this month. And a surprising number come from close to home – did you know that there are over 150 Christian martyrs from the U.S. and Canada, including eight from Virginia?

But although this list could go on and on, the thousands of saints officially listed by the Church are only a tiny fraction of the Christians who have ever lived. And on All Saints' Day, when we think about saints, and about what it means to be a saint, it's also good for us to remember that all of us – every Christian who is alive, not just a select few – every one of us is called to be a saint. Every one of us here, if we are who we were made to be, will end up where all those saints I've just mentioned are now – in heaven.

I want to say this a few different ways, because if we take this seriously, this idea can change the way we live our lives. The truth is, we should all be working to become saints.

How about this quote – it's from a controversial French writer named Leon Bloy. Bloy was a convert from atheism to Catholicism. He said, "Life holds only one tragedy: not to have been a saint." That has sometimes been reworded this way: the only tragedy in life is not to have been a saint.[62]

Do we believe this? When we die, do we want to die with the most toys? Or do we want to die and go to heaven? When we hear the names of saints the Church has recognized, do we think, am I doing what it takes to join them? I don't necessarily mean to join them as a face on a holy card, or to get our own day on the calendar, but to join them in heaven. One definition of a saint, as I said a moment ago, is someone who is in heaven. Are we living like that's our goal?

Here's another way to say this: you were made to be a saint. You might think, "no, I don't think so, not me. I was made to be a student or a teacher or a mechanic or a doctor or a nurse or a truck driver or an artist..." or whatever you do or hope to do one day with your life. But that role, that job that you think of as being important to who you are, if it's the right one for you, should also be your route to becoming a saint. Do what you are made to do and do it the way you should do it – and you're on the way to being a saint.

What might be a little scary is that it's our choice whether or not to be a saint. No one can make us do it. You don't have to be a nun or a bishop or a monk or a martyr to be a saint, though some well-known saints have been all those things. But you have to choose whether to be who you were made to be, or not. And being a saint is what we were made for, and when we're honest with ourselves, it's also what we really want. We don't want to be half-rate, half-finished, half-functional versions of ourselves. But the complete version of us, the ideal version of us, is the one that's meant to live with God forever – a saint.

If we're all made to live forever with God, then we're all made to be saints, so whatever we do now that prevents us from becoming more ready to live with God is contrary to what we really know is best for us. Too often we don't act like we believe that – but deep inside we know it's true, and when we're honest, we do want to be fully human, and completely ourselves, and the only way to do that is to become a saint.

I also said earlier that saints are holy. Maybe the words holy or holiness sound a little stuffy to you. When someone starts talking about holiness, you might brace yourself for a long list of do's and don'ts. But how about this definition: being holy is being fully, completely who God made you to be. Not what

---

[62] Quoted, among other places, in *Prayer for Beginners*, Peter Kreeft, 2000, Ignatius Press, p. 39.

society tries to tell you to be – but what God made you to be. You, and no one else. It involves a close relationship with Him. And the Church is here to help with that. The Beatitudes, the words of Jesus that we just heard, are guidelines for living like that.

Yes, that includes doing some things and not doing others. It includes pursuing the virtues and doing acts of mercy. But it also means doing those things in a way that is unique to you.

God is completely holy, and perfectly loving, and consistently merciful. In more than one place in the Bible God tells his people be holy, because I am holy. And as we become more holy, we're becoming more like God, and we're also becoming more like who we were meant to be.

People were made to live with God, but nothing unholy can enter the presence of God. So it only makes sense that we were made to be holy. Being anything less is being less than our potential, less than we were made to be. That doesn't mean that we should all look and act the same – in fact, holiness should look a little different in each one of us.

Often in life we find that worthwhile things take great effort, and I'm not saying that becoming a saint is easy. But all those many saints who we remember today are waiting for us to ask them to help us be who we should be.

So on All Saints Day we remember not only that there are many saints, but also that we're all meant to join them – to make the crowd much, much larger than it already is. And the Church has always promised that we can all get there. It's what we're all here for, and it's something we all have the potential for, each in our own way: to be all saints.

GROW UP!
1 John 3:2

Solemnity of All Saints, 1 Nov 2017

"Oh, grow up!" Have you ever said that to anyone? Has anyone ever said that to you? Why don't you grow up? Normally if we say that to someone, we're implying that they're acting like a child when they shouldn't. They're acting immature, but they should know better.

Children, on the other hand, we can expect to act like children. And we should expect them to act like children. And although physically speaking all of us here today are a lot of different ages, when it comes to God, we're all children. Our second reading says, "we are God's children now." John wrote that to some of the first Christians. Notice that he includes himself: he says, we are God's children, not you are God's children. This is one of the leaders of the early Church writing, yet he labels himself as a child.

If you've ever had children, or you've ever known children, or you've ever been a child – and I think that covers everyone, right? – then you know that children are, by definition, immature. Children don't always do what we want them to do. They don't always know what to do. No surprise, right? But as far as our lives as Christians are concerned, we're all children. One reason is because we all have the same Creator, the same Father in heaven. That will never change. But another reason is that, unless we're completely mature spiritually, we still act like children in our spiritual lives. And that can change.

In one way, being a child is meant to be temporary. We start as children, but then we grow up. More or less… some of us more, some of us less…. But also, we're always the children of our parents. No matter how old we get, we can't go back in time and change the fact that we are someone's children. And as Christians we can't change the fact that we're God's children. But we can ask ourselves if we act like we're his children, or if we ignore that basic truth about ourselves.

Being children is where we all start, physically. That's not a bad thing. But we're not meant to stay children in physical terms. Remember the story of Peter Pan? The boy who wouldn't grow up? Peter Pan was not the first boy who wouldn't grow up. The idea of the eternal youth goes back to classical mythology. But whether it's characters in ancient stories, or Peter Pan on stage or in a movie, they catch our attention because we know there's something unnatural about not growing up. There are strange things about these eternally young characters, things that I won't describe right now. They make for interesting stories, but in real life if we meet someone like that, we know something's not right. We know something would be unnatural about watching our friends and family get older while we don't. We know that the world doesn't really work that way.

And that's true in the spiritual life as well as the physical life. We get baptized, we receive communion, and we're confirmed – but that's just the beginning. We're still spiritual babies. And our spiritual growth isn't meant to stop with confirmation – it should just be getting started. Unlike physical growth, our spiritual growth isn't meant to stop until we die. And maybe not then. We don't keep getting taller and taller as we get older and older – but we should keep getting to know God better and better.

In the letter we heard from earlier, John says not only that we are God's children now, but also that "what we shall be has not yet been revealed." We aren't done growing yet. Does that mean we don't know where we're heading, or we don't know what mature Christians look like? No, it doesn't. We have thousands of models for what it means to be a grown-up Christian. We call them saints. And where they are is where we should be headed – heaven.

Today's feast is the Solemnity of All Saints, when we get to celebrate the great diversity of saints from all over the world, who give us many different models of what mature Christian life can be. They've spoken many different languages and had many different personalities. Some lived to be quite old, but others were children, or at least very young, when they died.

St. Thérèse of Lisieux was only 24 when she died, but because of her insight, Pope John Paul II, another great saint, recognized her as a Doctor of the Church. So it's remarkable that one-way St. Thérèse talked about getting closer to God was by embracing the fact that we are children when it comes to our relationship with Him. She wrote this: "I see that it is enough to recognize one's nothingness and to abandon oneself, like a child, into God's arms. ... I rejoice to be little because only children, and those who are like them, will be admitted to the heavenly banquet."[63]

---

[63] An excerpt from one of her letters that has been quoted often, e.g. in *The Gospel According to St. Thérèse*, Joseph F. Schmidt, F.S.C., 2017, The Word Among Us Press, p. 100. Thérèse's autobiography, *Story of a Soul*, is a spiritual classic, and contains more on the theme of spiritual childhood.

So to grow up spiritually, we have to remain children. It's a great paradox of our faith. We can't remain children physically. We should mature, physically and spiritually. But to mature spiritually, according to one great saint, means to recognize that in some way we will always be God's children. Accepting our childhood helps us mature spiritually. And we can't force spiritual growth on our own. We depend on God for it – because we are children, and children are dependent on their parents. And no matter how much we grow up, we will still always be God's children.

All the saints we remember today realizing that. They're in heaven with their heavenly Father – and ours. We can think of them as our older, more mature brothers and sisters who are waiting to help us. It only makes sense for us to pray to them – to say thank you, and to ask them to help us grow up.

NO EXCUSES FOR MARTIN
Luke 14:15-24

Memorial of Saint Martin de Porres, 3 Nov 2015

I don't know about you, but I'm probably better than I should be at making excuses when I don't want to do something. And as a teacher, I hear a lot of excuses – some good, some not so good.

In today's gospel, we hear some excuses. Some people have been invited to a feast, but they don't want to go. (I don't know why – a feast sounds like a good idea to me!) But they made excuses. The thing is, their excuses sound pretty good. Buying new property that needs inspection – that's what we might call a job-related excuse. Getting married – that's what we might call a family-related excuse. But it's clear from the parable that Jesus didn't think these excuses were good enough.

Today we're celebrating the feast of St. Martin de Porres. Martin was born in Lima, Peru, in 1579. And Martin had some pretty good excuses. He was born poor and grew up with a single mother. His father abandoned Martin and his mother and sister. He was a victim of racial prejudice because of his dark skin. His education was by our standards inadequate and incomplete.

But Martin did not let these excuses stop him from becoming a saint. Even as a young child he had a special concern for the poor and the sick, and he became famous for that. One story says that once his mother sent him to town with three coins to buy something for her. Along the way he met a beggar lady who had no food. Martin gave her the three coins and returned home happy that he'd been able to help the lady. His mother wasn't so happy.

Martin began to work with the Dominicans in Lima when he was 14 or 15 years old. He became a third order Dominican first, and then a lay brother. He studied basic medicine. He continued to help the poor, and sometimes still got in trouble for it. Once there was a plague in Lima, and the prior had told the Dominican friars not to bring any sick people into the priory. But one day Martin was walking home and found an Indian man who had been injured and was bleeding to death. Martin brought him to the priory and put him in his own bed. The prior reprimanded Martin when he found out.

Eventually Martin founded an orphanage and a hospital. By the time he died Martin had an international reputation as a healer. We also know that he lived a life of intense prayer. Despite all the good excuses he might have had not to, he became a saint. As we think about today's gospel, and as we remember Martin de Porres, it's a good time for us to ask: What's our excuse for not becoming a saint?

THE HUMILITY OF ST. CHARLES
Philippians 2:7-8

Memorial of Saint Charles Borromeo, 4 Nov 2014

Humility is a great Christian virtue. We're reminded today in our reading from Philippians that Jesus is our model of humility. Although Jesus was God, he humbled himself, came in human appearance, and died a human death of shame and misery. But we can't ignore what happened next: Jesus was raised from the dead following his humiliation, and ascended to heaven, and was glorified. This scriptural pattern – of humility followed by glorification – descent followed by ascent – is a pattern that's also found in the lives of the saints. Today we celebrate the life of Saint Charles Borromeo, who gives us an exceptional demonstration of saintly humility.

Charles Borromeo was born into a wealthy northern Italian family in 1538. His father was a count; his mother was a Medici and the older sister of Pope Pius IV. As a young man he was well-educated. He enjoyed hunting and playing the lute and cello. At age 21, his uncle the pope created him cardinal and made him administrator of the papal states. When his older brother died a few years later, his family expected him to take on more responsibility in managing family affairs and become less involved in the Church. But Charles decided to lay aside his wealth and to humble himself by seeking ordination and a life serving others.

He helped bring the Council of Trent to a successful close and was made Archbishop of Milan. Again, he was given status and power. Bishops at that time did not always live in their dioceses, but Charles believed they should. He convinced the pope to let him leave Rome and made himself an example by spending the rest of his life shepherding his people.

The family seal of the Borromeos included the Latin word *Humilitas* or humility. This word became Charles's emblem, and he attempted to live it out in his life as bishop. In art St. Charles is often shown with a rope around his neck; sometimes he walked through Milan barefoot and wearing a rope as a sign of humility. When the plague hit Milan he could have left, but he stayed, and is shown in many paintings administering sacraments to the dying.

Charles also worked to purge the Church of materialism; he guided reforms of several religious groups. One of these was ironically named the Humiliati, though many of the Humiliati lived lifestyles that were not notably humble. Some of them were so angry that they tried to have Charles killed, but when a hired assassin shot him in the back at point blank range, the bullet bounced off.

Charles died in 1584, at the age of 46, sick and exhausted from his work. He was canonized in 1610. He's recognized as the patron saint of catechists because he helped produce the *Catechism* of Trent, and he also reminds us that catechists have to humble themselves – to bring themselves down to the level of their students – so they can help their students rise up through education.

St. Charles is also frequently shown in art adoring Jesus in the Blessed Sacrament – appropriate since the Eucharist itself shows us the humility of Christ. Jesus humbled himself by becoming man, but by coming to us under the form of bread and wine He also shows humility, a willingness to expose himself to human misunderstanding, or even abuse.

Every saint is different, and everyone shows virtue in different ways. In following Jesus, St. Charles showed us humility in ways that fit his own life, in his own time and place. Remembering his life gives each of us an opportunity to ask: what role does humility play in my life? If we have hopes of becoming saints, as we should, we'll do well to consider this question.

St. Charles Borromeo – pray for us.

www.ingramcontent.com/pod-product-compliance
Lightning Source LLC
Chambersburg PA
CBHW072011110526
44592CB00012B/1266